(PHILIP LEVINE)

NEW
SELECTED
POEMS

BOOKS BY PHILIP LEVINE

THE SIMPLE TRUTH   1994

WHAT WORK IS   1991

NEW SELECTED POEMS   1991

A WALK WITH TOM JEFFERSON   1988

SWEET WILL   1985

SELECTED POEMS   1984

ONE FOR THE ROSE   1981

7 YEARS FROM SOMEWHERE   1979

ASHES: POEMS NEW AND OLD   1979

THE NAMES OF THE LOST   1976

1933   1974

THEY FEED THEY LION   1972

RED DUST   1971

PILI'S WALL   1971

NOT THIS PIG   1968

ON THE EDGE   1963

PHILIP LEVINE

NEW
SELECTED
POEMS

ALFRED A. KNOPF   NEW YORK   1997

THIS IS A BORZOI BOOK
PUBLISHED BY ALFRED A. KNOPF, INC.

Library of Congress Cataloging-in-Publication Data
Levine, Philip, 1928–
    [Selections, 1991]
    New selected poems / by Philip Levine. — 1st ed.
        p.   cm.
    ISBN 0-679-74056-2
    I. Title.
PS3562.E9A6   1991
811'.54—dc20   90-53422
                                                           CIP

Manufactured in the United States of America
First paperback edition published May 10, 1991
Reprinted Five Times
Seventh Printing, July 1997

THIS BOOK IS FOR FRAN

CONTENTS

Contents

FROM THEY FEED THEY LION *(1972)*

FROM 1933 *(1974)*

FROM THE NAMES OF THE LOST *(1976)*

Contents

FROM SWEET WILL *(1985)*

FROM A WALK WITH TOM JEFFERSON *(1988)*

FROM

ON THE EDGE

LIGHTS I HAVE SEEN BEFORE

The children are off somewhere
and when I waken
I hear only
the buzz of current
in the TV
and the refrigerator

groaning against the coming
day. I rise and wash;
there is nothing
to think of except
the insistent push
of water, and the pipe's

cry against the water. I
shave carefully,
wanting to say
something to someone,
wanting to ease
myself away from the face

that is faintly familiar.
Later, at my desk
a young girl
cries against the past
and the new world
she is afraid to enter.

She puts her head down, trying
to hide what I hear,
trying to ask
for understanding
and quiets, and leaves,
and leaves the memory of

no word I can understand. On
the way home houses

that are insane
spread on my left hand
and on my right.
I drive on the road between.

Between the cry of matter
and the cry of those
whose lives are here
what is there to choose
but failure? What
can one say to oneself that

will make it believable?
And I am on my
block, slowing for
clusters of children
who hear nothing.
My next-door neighbor sees me

and waves as I pass and goes
on chasing behind
the power mower
in a spray of grass
and lights come on
where I have seen them before.

FOR FRAN

She packs the flower beds with leaves,
Rags, dampened papers, ties with twine
The lemon tree, but winter carves
Its features on the uprooted stem.

I see the true vein in her neck
And where the smaller ones have broken
Blueing the skin, and where the dark
Cold lines of weariness have eaten

Out through the winding of the bone.
On the hard ground where Adam strayed,
Where nothing but his wants remain,
What do we do to those we need,

To those whose need of us endures
Even the knowledge of what we are?
I turn to her whose future bears
The promise of the appalling air,

My living wife, Frances Levine,
Mother of Theodore, John, and Mark,
Out of whatever we have been
We will make something for the dark.

MY POETS

One was put in the lockup
in Toledo, Ohio
for ever and ever. One
took up country banjo
and teamed with an over-sexed
inarticulate midget
on harmonica. One writes
from Memphis that the whole weight
of the South is killing him
and the gangrenous Baptists
won't let him piss in peace.

Another I loved has three
tailors—the bad Baudelaire
of South Pasadena, he
can't scream for fear of waking
the neighbors and watches TV
without sound and writes nothing.
And the nation calls for its soul,
calls for its blood and belly,
and we, we number the five
fingers of our fists and try
anything to stay alive
without poems.
                    Today on the
eve of Thanksgiving I said
I will close my eyes, girl-like,
and when I open them there
will be something here to love
and to celebrate. When I
opened them there was only
the blank door and beyond it
the hall, and I did not see
William Blake as a dark child
crying: "Without a Poet
dreamless you slept on the blue
floor of Atlantis till I

came with 27 words
& a hand opened by the
waters of the Ohio
& made you America."

L'HOMME ET LA BETE

It is summertime,
The hanging time,
Bread is dear
And last year's wine
Almost gone
And a poor harvest
Not yet in.
Three weeks ago
Mondre's sow
Ate a child.
The mother saw
This thing, and heard
The farrows squeal,
Too terrified
To share the meal.
Mother with infant,
Beggar and mayor
Pickpocket, pimp,
And the town whore
Have come to see
The infliction of
The court's decree.
A creaking wheel
Over the stones,
And drawn by a mule
The cart comes.
Squealing, head down,
With pinioned feet
Pushing in air
Against her fate,
The sow must hear
In a clerk's Latin
The stumbling sentence.
The drum is beaten,
The crowd hushed,
The sow stripped
Of the ragged dress,

Revealing whipped
And branded hams.
Now she is lifted
Up in air;
The noose catches
On her ear
But the hangman
Slips it down,
And again
Her feet are kicking.
Mondre shouts
That all may hear
He is glad
The end is near
For this mad
Rebellious sow.
Summer thickens;
The fly and the crow
Come to gather
All they can.
Soon the hard
Descending Fall.
Not on earth
And not in heaven,
The animal
Must slowly rot
With no good wishes
And one *bon mot*:
"In God's world
A pig receives
The ceremony
A pig deserves."

ON THE EDGE

My name is Edgar Poe and I was born
In 1928 in Michigan.
Nobody gave a damn. The gruel I ate
Kept me alive, nothing kept me warm,
But I grew up, almost to five foot ten,
And nothing in the world can change my weight.

I have been watching you these many years,
There in the office, pencil poised and ready,
Or on the highway when you went ahead.
I did not write; I watched you watch the stars
Believing that the wheel of fate was steady;
I saw you rise from love and go to bed;

I heard you lie, even to your daughter.
I did not write, for I am Edgar Poe,
Edgar the mad one, silly, drunk, unwise,
But Edgar waiting on the edge of laughter,
And there is nothing that he does not know
Whose page is blanker than the raining skies.

THE HORSE

for Ichiro Kawamoto, humanitarian,
electrician, & survivor of Hiroshima

They spoke of the horse alive
without skin, naked, hairless,
without eyes and ears, searching
for the stableboy's caress.
Shoot it, someone said, but they
let him go on colliding with
tattered walls, butting his long
skull to pulp, finding no path
where iron fences corkscrewed in
the street and bicycles turned
like question marks.
            Some fled and
some sat down. The river burned
all that day and into the
night, the stones sighed a moment
and were still, and the shadow
of a man's hand entered
a leaf.
            The white horse never
returned, and later they found
the stable boy, his back crushed
by a hoof, his mouth opened
around a cry that no one heard.

They spoke of the horse again
and again; their mouths opened
like the gills of a fish caught
above water.
            Mountain flowers
burst from the red clay walls, and
they said a new life was here.
Raw grass sprouted from the cobbles
like hair from a deafened ear.

The horse would never return.

There had been no horse. I could
tell from the way they walked
testing the ground for some cold
that the rage had gone out of
their bones in one mad dance.

NOT THIS PIG

A NEW DAY

The headlights fading out at dawn,
A stranger at the shore, the shore
Not wakening to the great sea
Out of sleep, and night, and no sun
Rising where it rose before.

The old champion in a sweat suit
Tells me this is Chicago, this—
He does not say—is not the sea
But the chopped grey lake you get to
After travelling all night

From Dubuque, Cairo, or Wyandotte.
He takes off at a slow trot
And the fat slides under his shirt.
I recall the Friday night
In a beer garden in Detroit

I saw him flatten Ezzard Charles
On TV, and weep, and raise
Both gloved hands in a slow salute
To a God. I could tell him that.
I could tell him that those good days

Were no more and no less than these.
I could tell him that I thought
By now I must have reached the sea
We read about, or that last night
I saw a man break down and cry

Out of luck and out of gas
In Bruce's Crossing. We collect
Here at the shore, the two of us,
To make a pact, a people come
For a new world and a new home

And what we get is what we bring:
A grey light coming on at dawn,
No fresh start and no bird song
And no sea and no shore
That someone hasn't seen before.

BLASTING FROM HEAVEN

The little girl won't eat her sandwich;
she lifts the bun and looks in, but the grey beef
coated with relish is always there.
Her mother says, "Do it for mother."
Milk and relish and a hard bun that comes off
like a hat—a kid's life is a cinch.

And a mother's life? "What can you do
with a man like that?" she asks the sleeping cook
and then the old Negro who won't sit.
"He's been out all night trying to get it.
I hope he gets it. What did he ever do
but get it?" The Negro doesn't look,

though he looks like he's been out all night
trying. Everyone's been out all night trying.
Why else would we be drinking beer
at attention? If she were younger,
or if I were Prince Valiant, I would say that fate
brought me here to quiet the crying,

to sweeten the sandwich of the child,
to waken the cook, to stop the Negro from
bearing witness to the world. The dawn
still hasn't come, and now we hear
the 8 o'clock whistles blasting from heaven,
and with no morning the day is sold.

TO A CHILD TRAPPED IN A
BARBER SHOP

You've gotten in through the transom
and you can't get out
till Monday morning or, worse,
till the cops come.

That six-year-old red face
calling for mama
is yours; it won't help you
because your case

is closed forever, hopeless.
So don't drink
the Lucky Tiger, don't
fill up on grease

because that makes it a lot worse,
that makes it a crime
against property and the state
and that costs time.

We've all been here before,
we took our turn
under the electric storm
of the vibrator

and stiffened our wills to meet
the close clippers
and heard the true blade mowing
back and forth

on a strip of dead skin,
and we stopped crying.
You think your life is over?
It's just begun.

THE CEMETERY AT
ACADEMY, CALIFORNIA

On a hot summer Sunday
I came here with my children
who wandered among headstones
kicking up dust clouds. They found
a stone that said DAVI and
nothing more, and beneath the stone
a dead gopher, flat and dry.
Later they went off to play
on the dry dirt hills; I napped
under a great tree and woke
surprised by three teenagers.
They had put flowers in tin cans
around a headstone that showed
the sunrise over a slate sea,
and in the left-hand corner
a new bronze dove broke for peace.
Off in the distance my boys
had discovered the outhouses,
the twin whitewashed sentinels,
and were unwinding toilet
paper and dropping whatever
they could find through the dark holes,
and when I found and scolded
them the two younger ones squeezed
my hands and walked stiffly at
my side past the three mourners.

I came here with a young girl
once who perched barefoot on her
family marker. "I will go
there," she said, "next to my sister."
It was early morning and
cold, and I wandered over
the pale clodded ground looking
for something rich or touching.
"It's all wildflowers in the spring,"

she had said, but in July
there were only the curled cut
flowers and the headstones blanked out
on the sun side, and the long
shadows deep as oil. I walked
to the sagging wire fence
that marked the margin of the
place and saw where the same ground,
festered here and there with reedy
grass, rose to a small knoll
and beyond where a windmill
held itself against the breeze.
I could hear her singing on
the stone under the great oak,
but when I got there she was
silent and I wasn't sure
and was ashamed to ask her,
ashamed that I had come here
where her people turned the earth.

Yet I came again, alone,
in the evening when the leaves
turned in the heat toward darkness
so late in coming. There was
her sister, there was her place
undisturbed, relatives and
friends, and other families
spread along the crests of this
burned hill. When I kneeled
to touch the ground it seemed like
something I had never seen,
the way the pale lumps broke down
to almost nothing, nothing
but the source of what they called
their living. She, younger now
than I, would be here some day

beneath the ground my hand combed.
The first night wind caught the leaves
above, crackling, and on
the trunk a salamander
faded in the fading light.
One comes for answers to a
place like this and finds even
in the darkness, even in
the sudden flooding of the
headlights, that in time one comes
to be a stranger to nothing.

SILENT IN AMERICA

"Vivas for those who have failed . . ."

I
Since I no longer speak I
go unnoticed among men;
in the far corners of rooms,
greeted occasionally
with a stiff wave, I am seen
aslant as one sees a pane

of clear glass, reflecting both
what lies before and behind
in a dazzle of splendid
approximations. They mouth
to each other, and the wind
answers them, while my tongue, furred,

captive, wandering between
contagious wards of the palate,
discovers a foreignness
that is native. One woman,
hearing me grunt for breath, sits
by my side in a green dress,

her hands cupped in the valley
of her life. She would receive
my sympathy and in my
eyes sees—God knows what she sees
in my eyes. Let them have
all they find under the sky.

II
Sometimes on especially
    warm evenings I
take a card chair out under
    the almond tree

and catching the last light, speak
    to myself without
words. I try to catch what is
    behind my throat,

without words, all that exists
    behind and before.
Under the low branches the
    earth's matted floor,

cropped Bermuda and clover
    that the bees attack,
glistens in shade. The sprinkler
    swings out of dark

into light and back again,
    and the water sighs
as though it were suffering
    before my own eyes.

Before my own eyes I am
    almost speaking; my
jaws ache for release, for
    words that will say

anything. I force myself
    to remember
who I am, what I am, and
    why I am here.

III
    When Dr. Leo
addresses me, I pretend
    to be distracted:
    "Look here, Philip, no
damage," and he points his wand
    at a clogged bridgehead

in the white-on-black
map of my throat. The lights come
on again. I blink
like a good patient.
Behind two great stained thumbs
he advances straight

toward my defenseless
mouth, enters and pries. The hair
on his hands interests
me no longer, nor
does his magic power amaze.
He has his good days

and his bad. I see
from her gold breast-pin nursey's
a grade A typist,
and he, from his acts,
is an existentialist
with no faith in facts.

IV

And I, I am the silent
riser in a house
of garrulous children.
I am Fresno's

dumb bard, America's last
hope, sheep in sheep's
clothing. Who names the past
names me, who sleeps

by my side shall find despair
and happiness,
a twi-night double header.
He who loves less

than I, loves no one, who speaks
  more than I, speaks
too much, I am everything
  that is dishonest,

everything under the sun.
  And I say "balls,"
the time will never come
  nor ripeness be all.

v
    I tell time
by the sunlight's position
  on the bedroom wall:
it's 5:30, middle June.
    I rise, dress,
    assume my name

    and feel my
face against a hard towel.
  My mind is empty;
I see all that's here to see:
    the garden
    and the hard sky;

    the great space
between the two has a weight,
  a reality
which I find is no burden,
    and the height
    of the cot tree

    is only
what it has come to deserve.
  I have not found peace,

but I have found I am where
I am by
being only there,

by standing
in the clouded presence of
the things I observe.
What is it in the air or the
water caught
on the branches

of the brown
roses hanging toward autumn?
What is it that moves
when it's still, and strikes me dumb
when it speaks
of being alive.

VI

In a room with no way out,
abandoned by everyone
to something they call my fate,
with only my squat demon,
my little Bobby, jumping up
and down, demanding women,
demanding more in his cup,
pushing his hand where a hand

should not be pushed, pushing his
shrill voice everywhere, I tried
escape, but the broken stairs
went nowhere. "Police," I cried,
but the phones were off the hook,
and I wasn't, and Bobby
was close behind with a trick
or two up his sleeve, his fly

catching like canvas on the
night wind, crying, "One more, just one."
Knowing he would master me,
I turned to you: "Levine,"
I called softly, and called you
again and again, and it was I who,
given unto Bobby, screamed NO.

VII
For a black man whose
name I have forgotten who danced
all night at Chevy
Gear & Axle,
for that great stunned Pole
who laughed when he called me Jew
Boy, for the ugly
who had no chance,

the beautiful in
body, the used and the unused,
those who had courage
and those who quit—
Rousek and Ficklin
numbed by their own self-praise
who ate their own shit
in their own rage;

for these and myself
whom I loved and hated, I
had presumed to speak
in measure.
The great night is half
over, and the stage is dark;
all my energy,
all my care for

those I cannot touch
runs on my breath like a sigh;
surely I have failed.
My own wife
and my children reach
in their sleep for some sure sign,
but each has his life
private and sealed.

VIII

I speak to H. in a bar
in downtown L.A.
Over a schooner of beer
he waits out the day
in the anonymous dark.
Archimbault is here—
I do not have to be drunk
to feel him come near,

and he touches me with his
life, and I could cry,
though I don't know who he is
or why I should care
about the mad ones, imagined
and real, H. places
in his cherished underground,
their wounded faces

glowing in the half-light of
their last days alive,
as his glows here. Let me have
the courage to live
as fictions live, proud, careless,
unwilling to die.
We pay for our drinks, rise,
and enter the city

waiting, impatient and loud.
 Come with us tonight,
drifters in the drifting crowd,
 we shall arrive, late
and tired, beyond the false lights
 of Pasadena
where the living are silent
 in America.

THE MIDGET

In this café Durruti,
the unnamable, plotted
the burning of the Bishop
of Zaragoza, or so
the story goes. Now it's a hot
tourist spot in season, but
in mid-December the bar
is lined with factory workers
and day laborers as gray
as cement. The place smells
of cement and of urine,
and no one takes off his coat
or sits down to his sherry—
a queen's drink, as thin and dry
as benzine.
              It is Sunday,
late, and each man drinks alone,
seriously. Down the bar
a midget sings to himself,
sings of how from the starving South
he came, a boy, to this terrible
Barcelona, and ate. Not
all the songs are for himself;
he steps back from the bar,
his potbelly pushed out
and wrapped intricately
in a great, somber cummerbund,
and tells the world who is big,
big in the heart, and big down
here, big where it really counts.

Now he comes over to me,
and it is for me he sings.
Does he want money? I try
to buy him off with a drink,
a bored smile, but again
I hear of his power, of how

the Germans, Dutch, English—all
the world's babies—come to him,
and how on the fields of skin
he struts. "Here," he says to me,
"feel this and you'll believe."

In a voice suddenly thin
and adolescent, I tell him
I believe. "Feel this, feel this . . ."
I turn away from him, but
he turns with me, and the room
freezes except for us two.
I can smell the bitterness
of his sweat, and from the cracked
corners of his eyes see the tears
start down their worn courses.
I say, No, No more! He tugs
at my sleeve, hulking now, and
too big for his little feet;
he tugs and will not let go,
and the others along the bar
won't turn or interfere
or leave their drinks. He gets
my hand, first my forefinger
like a carrot in his fist,
and then with the other hand,
my wrist, and at last I can't
shake him off or defend
myself.
　　　　He sits in my lap
and sings of Americas,
of those who never returned
and those who never left. The smell
of anise has turned his breath
to a child's breath, but his cheeks,
stiff and peeling, have started
to die. They have turned along

the bar to behold me
on the raised throne of a torn
plastic barstool, blank and drunk
and half asleep. One by one
with the old curses thrown down
they pay up and go out,
and though the place is still
except for the new rumbling
of the morning catching fire
no one hears or no one cares
that I sing to this late-born freak
of the old world swelling my lap,
I sing lullaby, and sing.

HEAVEN

If you were twenty-seven
and had done time for beating
your ex-wife and had
no dreams you remembered
in the morning, you might
lie on your bed and listen
to a mad canary sing
and think it all right to be
there every Saturday
ignoring your neighbors, the streets,
the signs that said join,
and the need to be helping.
You might build, as he did,
a network of golden ladders
so that the bird could roam
on all levels of the room;
you might paint the ceiling blue,
the floor green, and shade
the place you called the sun
so that things came softly to order
when the light came on.
He and the bird lived
in the fine weather of heaven;
they never aged, they
never tired or wanted
all through that war,
but when it was over
and the nation had been saved,
he knew they'd be hunted.
He knew, as you would too,
that he'd be laid off
for not being braver,
and it would do no good
to show how he had taken
clothespins and cardboard
and made each step safe.
It would do no good

to have been one of the few
that climbed higher and higher
even in time of war,
for now there would be the poor
asking for their share,
and hurt men in uniforms,
and no one to believe
that heaven was really here.

WAKING AN ANGEL

Sparrows quarreled outside our window,
roses swelled, the cherry boughs burst
into fire, and it was spring

in the middle of a bad winter.
We have been good, she said, we have
avoided the fields, tended

our private affairs without complaint,
and this is surely our reward.
I wasn't so sure. There were

hard grey spots on the underbelly
of the ring-tailed coon that died
in the garbage, there was sand

as white as powdered glass overflowing
the vessel of the hyacinth,
there was sand on my own tongue

when I awakened at one or two
in the dark, my nostrils inflamed,
my voice crying out for her.

She wouldn't move. I put my cold hands
on her hips and rocked her gently;
O, O, O was all she said

through set, dry lips. She was slipping
away from me. I was afraid to look
at what dense wings lifted her

out of my bedroom and my one life,
her voice still trailing O, O, O,
like a raiment of victory.

ANIMALS ARE PASSING
FROM OUR LIVES

It's wonderful how I jog
on four honed-down ivory toes
my massive buttocks slipping
like oiled parts with each light step.

I'm to market. I can smell
the sour, grooved block, I can smell
the blade that opens the hole
and the pudgy white fingers

that shake out the intestines
like a hankie. In my dreams
the snouts drool on the marble,
suffering children, suffering flies,

suffering the consumers
who won't meet their steady eyes
for fear they could see. The boy
who drives me along believes

that any moment I'll fall
on my side and drum my toes
like a typewriter or squeal
and shit like a new housewife

discovering television,
or that I'll turn like a beast
cleverly to hook his teeth
with my teeth. No. Not this pig.

BABY VILLON

He tells me in Bangkok he's robbed
Because he's white; in London because he's black;
In Barcelona, Jew; in Paris, Arab:
Everywhere and at all times, and he fights back.

He holds up seven thick little fingers
To show me he's rated seventh in the world,
And there's no passion in his voice, no anger
In the flat brown eyes flecked with blood.

He asks me to tell all I can remember
Of my father, his uncle; he talks of the war
In North Africa and what came after,
The loss of his father, the loss of his brother,

The windows of the bakery smashed and the fresh bread
Dusted with glass, the warm smell of rye
So strong he ate till his mouth filled with blood.
"Here they live, here they live and not die,"

And he points down at his black head ridged
With black kinks of hair. He touches my hair,
Tells me I should never disparage
The stiff bristles that guard the head of the fighter.

Sadly his fingers wander over my face,
And he says how fair I am, how smooth.
We stand to end this first and last visit.
Stiff, 116 pounds, five feet two,

No bigger than a girl, he holds my shoulders,
Kisses my lips, his eyes still open,
My imaginary brother, my cousin,
Myself made otherwise by all his pain.

FROM
RED DUST

CLOUDS

I

Dawn. First light tearing
at the rough tongues of the zinnias,
at the leaves of the just born.

Today it will rain. On the road
black cars are abandoned, but the clouds
ride above, their wisdom intact.

They are predictions. They never matter.
The jet fighters lift above the flat roofs,
black arrowheads trailing their future.

II

When the night comes small fires go out.
Blood runs to the heart and finds it locked.

Morning is exhaustion, tranquilizers, gasoline,
the screaming of frozen bearings,
the failures of will, the tv talking to itself.

The clouds go on eating oil, cigars,
housewives, sighing letters,
the breath of lies. In their great silent pockets
they carry off all our dead.

III

The clouds collect until there's no sky.
A boat slips its moorings and drifts
toward the open sea, turning and turning.

The moon bends to the canal and bathes
her torn lips, and the earth goes on
giving off her angers and sighs

and who knows or cares except these
breathing the first rains,
the last rivers running over iron.

IV

You cut an apple in two pieces
and ate them both. In the rain
the door knocked and you dreamed it.
On bad roads the poor walked under cardboard boxes.

The houses are angry because they're watched.
A soldier wants to talk with God
but his mouth fills with lost tags.

The clouds have seen it all, in the dark
they pass over the graves of the forgotten
and they don't cry or whisper.

They should be punished every morning,
they should be bitten and boiled like spoons.

NOON

I bend to the ground
to catch
something whispered,
urgent, drifting
across the ditches.
The heaviness of
flies stuttering
in orbit, dirt
ripening, the sweat
of eggs.
      There are
small streams
the width of a thumb
running in the villages
of sheaves, whole
eras of grain
wakening on
the stalks, a roof
that breathes over
my head.
      Behind me
the tracks creaking
like a harness,
an abandoned bicycle
that cries and cries,
a bottle of common
wine that won't
pour.
At such times
I expect the earth
to pronounce. I say,
"I've been waiting
so long."
      Up ahead
a stand of eucalyptus
guards the river,
the river moving

east, the heavy light
sifts down driving
the sparrows for
cover, and the women
bow as they slap
the life out
of sheets and pants
and worn hands.

HOLDING ON

Green fingers
holding the hillside,
mustard whipping in
the sea winds, one blood-bright
poppy breathing in
and out. The odor
of Spanish earth comes
up to me, yellowed
with my own piss.

                                  40 miles from Málaga
half the world away
from home, I am home and
nowhere, a man who envies
grass.

           Two oxen browse
yoked together in the green clearing
below. Their bells cough. When
the darkness and the wet roll in
at dusk they gather
their great slow bodies toward
the stalls.

           If my spirit
descended now, it would be
a lost gull flaring against
a deepening hillside, or an angel
who cries too easily, or a single
glass of seawater, no longer blue
or mysterious, and still salty.

FIST

Iron growing in the dark,
it dreams all night long
and will not work. A flower
that hates God, a child
tearing at itself, this one
closes on nothing.

Friday, late,
Detroit Transmission. If I live
forever, the first clouded light
of dawn will flood me
in the cold streams
north of Pontiac.

It opens and is no longer.
Bud of anger, kinked
tendril of my life, here
in the forged morning
fill with anything—water,
light, blood—but fill.

HOW MUCH CAN IT HURT?

The woman at the checkstand
Who wishes you cancer

The fat man who hates his mother
The doctor who forgets

The soup bubbling on the back of the stove
The stone staring into the sun

The girl who kisses her own arms
The girl who fries her hair

The egg turning brown under the spoon
The lemon laughing all night long

My brother in his uniform over Dresden
The single thrill of fire going for the bed

The kindergarten blowing its windows out
Chalk burning the little fingers

The newspaper waiting all weekend
Dozing in rain with the deaths smeared on its lips

The oiling and loading and the springing
The bullets sucking quietly in their cradles

How much can it hurt in the wood
In the long nerve of lead, in the fattened head

How much can it hurt
In each ration of meat hooked and hanging

In the unfinished letter, the dried opened socket
The veil of skin flapping, the star falling

How Much Can It Hurt?

My face punctured with glass
The teeth eating themselves in dreams

Our blood refusing to breathe, refusing to sleep
Asking the wounded moon

Asking the pillow, asking, asking
How much can it hurt?

THE HELMET

All the way
on the road to Gary
he could see
where the sky shone
just out of reach
and smell the rich
smell of work
as strong as money,
but when he got there
the night was over.

People were going
to work and back,
the sidewalks were lakes
no one walked on,
the diners were saying
time to eat
so he stopped
and talked to a woman
who'd been up late
making helmets.

There are white hands
the color of steel,
they have put their lives
into steel,
and if hands could lay down
their lives these hands
would be helmets.
He and the woman
did not lie down

not because
she would praise
the steel helmet
boarding a train
for no war,

not because
he would find
the unjewelled crown
in a surplus store
where hands were sold.

They did not lie down
face to face
because of the waste
of being so close
and they were too tired
of being each other
to try to be lovers
and because they had
to sit up straight
so they could eat.

RED DUST

This harpie with dry red curls
talked openly of her husband,
his impotence, his death, the death
of her lover, the birth and death
of her own beauty. She stared
into the mirror next to
our table littered with the wreck
of her appetite and groaned:
Look what you've done to me!
as though only that moment
she'd discovered her own face.
Look, and she shoved the burden
of her ruin on the waiter.

I do not believe in sorrow;
it is not American.
At 8,000 feet the towns
of this blond valley smoke
like the thin pipes of the Chinese,
and I go higher where the air
is clean, thin, and the underside
of light is clearer than the light.
Above the tree line the pines
crowd below like moments of the past
and on above the snow line
the cold underside of my arm,
the half in shadow, sweats with fear
as though it lay along the edge
of revelation.

And so my mind closes around
a square oil can crushed on the road
one morning, startled it was not
the usual cat. If a crow
had come out of the air to choose
its entrails could I have laughed?
If eagles formed now in the

shocked vegetation of my sight
would they be friendly? I can hear
their wings lifting them down, the feathers
tipped with red dust, that dust which
even here I taste, having eaten it
all these years.

HOW MUCH EARTH

Torn into light, you woke wriggling
on a woman's palm. Halved, quartered,
shredded to the wind, you were the life
that thrilled along the underbelly
of a stone. Stilled in the frozen pond
you rinsed heaven with a sigh.

How much earth is a man.
A wall lies down and roses
rush from its teeth; in the fists
of the hungry, cucumbers sleep
their lives away, under your nails
the ocean moans in its bed.

How much earth.
The great ice fields slip
and the broken veins of an eye
startle under light, a hand is planted
and the grave blooms upward
in sunlight and walks the roads.

A SLEEPLESS NIGHT

April, and the last of the plum blossoms
scatters on the black grass
before dawn. The sycamore, the lime,
the struck pine inhale
the first pale hints of sky.
                              An iron day,
I think, yet it will come
dazzling, the light
rise from the belly of leaves and pour
burning from the cups
of poppies.
                              The mockingbird squawks
from his perch, fidgets,
and settles back. The snail, awake
for good, trembles from his shell
and sets sail for China. My hand dances
in the memory of a million vanished stars.

A man has every place to lay his head.

TOLD

The air lay softly on the green fur
of the almond, it was April

and I said, I begin again
but my hands burned in the damp earth

the light ran between my fingers
a black light like no other

this was not home, the linnet
settling on the oleander

the green pod swelling
the leaf slowly untwisting

the slashed egg fallen from the nest
the tongue of grass tasting

I was being told by a pulse slowing
in the eyes

the dove mourning in shadow
a nerve waking in the groin

the distant hills
turning their white heads away

told by the clouds assembling
in the trees, told by the blooming

of a black mouth beneath the rose
the worm sobbing, the dust

settling on my eyelid, told
by salt, by water, told and told.

PILI'S WALL

PILI'S WALL

I

Why me?

From this small hill
the river flows in March.
The soil gives grudgingly
grass, thyme, poppies,
thistles, cactus,
an olive grove climbing
the far hill, a row
of cedars shading the river.
What more?
A hobbled burro munching,
a she goat crying
for her young
who come crashing through
the tortured canyon.

What more?

II

I am the one
you never drew
the small sister
jumping rope
just within the circle
of the cypress

the lost dog
howling at shadows
and fleeing the chatter
of stones

the shepherd
alone and herdless

who came one afternoon
sweat running
from his eyes

seven jackdaws
soundless, until the sky
darkened
and there was
no place

III

Why am I here?
cries the gorse

Take these needles
crowding to your blood

these dense yellow mouths.
Take me, take me

the mother of spines
here under the olive

What can a child know,
says the moon

Look at her bones,
unbroken, and her teeth

May she sleep with stones
may she waken round a stone

Help me, help me may she help me
flaps the gull

far from the sea and drunk
on the air of sweet grass

IV

Black circle of the sun.
Legs that carry nothing.
Arms that hold still.

Here is a face for you
who will not show
your face.
    I cut a smile
and give it to you, the rain
gives you tears.

Cold hills of February,
a dark smudge of sky
crashing like a wall.

Black circle of the sun,
you sweat and freeze
by turns.
    Bark back.
Your face peels down
to the black bone.

Spit your teeth
in the face
of creation.

V

This is my hand
reaching to you.

There is the dark island
where it never cries.

You're bigger than me
so put your hand
on my shoulder.

Now we're together
in the green tunnel
of the spring.

Jonquils, mustard,
new leaves dusting the light,
bone white buttons

that let the fields
lift easily
in the wind.

And my hand
in yours.

VI

This is me.
As I am.

There is no child
inside me. I
am a child.

I am inside me
squeezed tight, the
bright tongue

of the thistle
at night

or the quick eyes

of a rabbit
or the one eye
of fire.

With long black hair
I'm shaking inside
me, unfolding

like a tree
turning and
turning

like a hand
in water or a widow
lost on the road.

VII

I press my hand over
my mouth, I see nothing.

A blood bean
leaps at the foot of the wall

and I am with my face
turned in.

Out of lime
out of thatch, straw, stones

out of the years
of peeling and crying

Out of saying No
No to the barn swallow, No

to the hurled stone
No to the air

out of you can't
to the crying grain, you won't

to the lost river
of blackening ivy

out of blind
out of deaf, closed, still

I stand and stand and stand into
this wall.

VIII

A simple dawn.

Inside the stalls
the pigs snuffle awake.
Light sifts through the thatch
crowning the dark odors,
the flies swing
in a rumor of birth
and the world starts.

From the far hill
of olives the wall is white
and perfect in the new sun.
The low houses of the poor
are squares of bread
dazzling the birds, and
no one can hear
the lost shoe
screaming in the weeds.

IX

Today I am
the wall, but once
I was seed

huddling between the grains
of stones, drawing a tongue

of salt into my blood, a fist
tightening into
a turnip

with one hard eye, until
a point of light
warmed

and gathering broke the dried crust
I was, and I was into
the air

the stiff back of me humping and
I breathed in
the green morning

like a row of windless corn
never to be
eaten.

X

Today I am Pili.
Palm Sunday, and I wait
in the cool morning

for my sisters, each one

in white to come
from the beaded door.

My brothers, restless, stone
the young pigs
into the road.

Below, the town trumpets
and I seem
to listen, I seem

to be this girl, this Pili, waiting
for children
with particular names

to gather before the chipped wall
and descend along
the goat trail,

and that is the sky up above, old father,
that seems to
be smiling down

on all of us with particular names, and that
is a field of cane,
there, across the road

where the pigs won't run
and a long dense shadow sleeps
at the roots.

FROM

THEY FEED
THEY LION

RENAMING THE KINGS

River of green stone,
in August '62 I stuck my head in
your lap one mile south of Piedra
where you fall suddenly away
from the highway. 107
in the valley and me
going dizzy, stopped the bike
and stumbled down
over the flat, patient stone, leaned out,
and then you in my eyes,
green tatters of memory, glimpses
of my own blood flashing
like fish, the grasses
dancing calmly, one silver point
like the charmed eye of an eel.
Five hours later I wakened
with the first darkness flowing
from the river bottom
through me to stone, to
the yellow land grasses and storming
the lower branches of the eucalyptus.
I could feel the water
draining from my blood and the stone
going out—the twin bushes of the lungs
held themselves seriously
like people about to take fire,
and when the first minnows startled
I rose into the sky. We
gathered every last tendril
of blue into our breath.

I named the stone John
after my mysterious second born.
High in its banks, slashed with silver,
riding the jagged blade of heaven
down to earth, the river shouts its name.

TO A FISH HEAD FOUND ON THE BEACH NEAR MÁLAGA

I

Flat, eventless afternoon
searching among the stones for nothing
I come upon the fish head.

                              "¡Hola!"
Right off, head to head, with this
wide-eyed, unlistening remnant
of dead metal trailing its single
stiff feather of flesh.

                    We talk of loneliness,
of the fear of stones falling like rain,
hatred of water tumbling out of dreams
and filling our small rooms. Shafts of sand
sifting under doors, filming
first the glasses, then the eyes,
weighing down the lips, the cry.

II

                              Here, halfway
from home, I discover my head, its hideous
King Tongue going. My good hands explore it,
the hair thinning, the eyes scratched
and hot, that let the lids thump down,
and the poor muscles, unsleeping,
as burned as drawn ropes.
Only the chin happy, hidden in fur.

III

But how good to find companionship
of any kind. Fish head and man head,
communing in their tongue, an iron yawn
out over the waves, the one poem born
of the eternal and always going back.
I throw the fish head to the sea.
Let it be fish once more.

                    I sniff my fingers

and catch the burned essential oil
seeping out of death. Out of beginning,
I hear, under the sea roar, the bone words
of teeth tearing earth and sea,
anointing the tongues with stone and sand,
water eating fish, fish water,
head eating head to let us be.

SALAMI

Stomach of goat, crushed
sheep balls, soft full
pearls of pig eyes,
snout gristle, fresh earth,
worn iron of trotter, slate
of Zaragoza, dried cat heart,
cock claws. She grinds
them with one hand and
with the other fists
mountain thyme, basil,
paprika, and knobs of garlic.
And if a tooth of stink thistle
pulls blood from the round
blue marbled hand
all the better for
this ruby of Pamplona,
this bright jewel of Vich,
this stained crown
of Solsona, this
salami.
            The daughter
of mismatched eyes,
36 year old infant smelling
of milk. Mama, she cries, mama,
but mama is gone,
and the old stone cutter
must wipe the drool
from her jumper. His puffed fingers
unbutton and point her
to toilet. Ten, twelve hours
a day, as long as the winter sun
holds up he rebuilds
the unvisited church
of San Martín. Cheep cheep
of the hammer high above
the town, sparrow cries
lost in the wind or lost

in the mind. At dusk he leans
to the coal dull wooden Virgin
and asks for blessings on
the slow one and peace
on his grizzled head, asks
finally and each night
for the forbidden, for
the knowledge of every
mysterious stone, and
the words go out on
the overwhelming incense
of salami.
            A single crow
passed high over the house,
I wakened out of nightmare.
The winds had changed,
the Tramontana was tearing
out of the Holy Mountains
to meet the sea winds
in my yard, burning and
scaring the young pines.
The single poplar wailed
in terror. With salt,
with guilt, with the need
to die, the vestments
of my life flared, I
was on fire, a stranger
staggering through my house
butting walls and falling
over furniture, looking
for a way out. In the last room
where moonlight slanted
through a broken shutter
I found my smallest son
asleep or dead, floating
on a bed of colorless light.
When I leaned closer

Salami

I could smell the small breaths
going and coming, and each
bore its prayer for me,
the true and earthy prayer
of salami.

COMING HOME, *Detroit*, 1968

A winter Tuesday, the city pouring fire,
Ford Rouge sulfurs the sun, Cadillac, Lincoln,
Chevy gray. The fat stacks
of breweries hold their tongues. Rags,
papers, hands, the stems of birches
dirtied with words.
                                    Near the freeway
you stop and wonder what came off,
recall the snowstorm where you lost it all,
the wolverine, the northern bear, the wolf
caught out, ice and steel raining
from the foundries in a shower
of human breath. On sleds in the false sun
the new material rests. One brown child
stares and stares into your frozen eyes
until the lights change and you go
forward to work. The charred faces, the eyes
boarded up, the rubble of innards, the cry
of wet smoke hanging in your throat,
the twisted river stopped at the color of iron.
We burn this city every day.

DETROIT GREASE SHOP POEM

Four bright steel crosses,
universal joints, plucked
out of the burlap sack—
"the heart of the drive train,"
the book says. Stars
on Lemon's wooden palm,
stars that must be capped,
rolled, and annointed,
that have their orders
and their commands as he
has his.

　　　　　　Under the blue
hesitant light another day
at Automotive
in the city of dreams.
We're all here to count
and be counted, Lemon,
Rosie, Eugene, Luis,
and me, too young to know
this is for keeps, pinning
on my apron, rolling up
my sleeves.

　　　　　　The roof leaks
from yesterday's rain,
the waters gather above us
waiting for one mistake.
When a drop falls on Lemon's
corded arm, he looks at it
as though it were something
rare or mysterious
like a drop of water or
a single lucid meteor
fallen slowly from
nowhere and burning on
his skin like a tear.

SATURDAY SWEEPING

Saturday sweeping
with an old broom
counting the strokes
back and forth.
The dust sprays
up silver in the
February sun
and comes down gray.
Soft straw muzzle
poking in and
bringing out
scraps of news,
little fingers
and signatures.
Everybody's
had this room
one time or another
and never thought
to sweep. Outside
the snows stiffen,
the roofs loosen
their last teeth
into the streets.
Outside it's
1952,
Detroit, unburned,
stumbles away
from my window
over the drained roofs
toward the river
to scald its useless
hands. Half
the men in this town
are crying in
the snow, their eyes
blackened like
Chinese soldiers.

The gates are closing
at Dodge Main
and Wyandotte
Chemical; they
must go home
to watch the kids
scrub their brown
faces or grease
cartridges for
the show down.
If anyone knocks
on your door
he'll be
oil flecked or
sea born, he'll
be bringing word
from the people
of the ice drifts
or the great talking dogs
that saved the Jews.
Meanwhile our masters
will come on
television
to ask for our help.
Here, the radiator's
working, stove says
Don't touch,
and the radio's crying,
I don't get enough.
I'm my keeper,
the only thing
I've got,
sweeping out
my one-room life
while the sun's
still up.

ANGEL BUTCHER

At sun up I am up
hosing down the outdoor abattoir
getting ready. The water
steams and hisses on the white stones
and the air pales to a
thin blue.
                    Today it is
Christophe. I don't see him
come up the long climb or
know he's here until I hear
my breathing double
and he's beside me smiling
like a young girl.
                    He asks
me the names of all
the tools and all
their functions, he lifts
and weighs and
balances, and runs a long
forefinger down the tongue
of each blade.
                    He asks
me how I came to this place and
this work, and I tell him how
I began with animals, and
he tells me how
he began with animals. We
talk about growing up and losing
the strange things we never
understood and settling.
                    I help
him with his robes; he
has a kind of modesty and sits
on the stone table with
the ends of the gown crossed
in his lap.
                    He wants to die

like a rabbit, and he wants me
to help him. I hold
his wrist; it's small, like
the throat of a young hen, but
cool and dry. He holds
mine and I can feel the
blood thudding in the ring
his fingers make.

He helps me, he
guides my hand at first. I can
feel my shoulders settle and
the bones take the weight, I can
feel my lungs flower as the
swing begins. He smiles again
with only one side of his mouth
and looks down to the
dark valley where the cities
burn. When I hit
him he comes apart like a
perfect puzzle or an
old flower.

And my legs
dance and twitch for hours.

THEY FEED THEY LION

Out of burlap sacks, out of bearing butter,
Out of black bean and wet slate bread,
Out of the acids of rage, the candor of tar,
Out of creosote, gasoline, drive shafts, wooden dollies,
They Lion grow.
                    Out of the gray hills
Of industrial barns, out of rain, out of bus ride,
West Virginia to Kiss My Ass, out of buried aunties,
Mothers hardening like pounded stumps, out of stumps,
Out of the bones' need to sharpen and the muscles' to stretch,
They Lion grow.
                    Earth is eating trees, fence posts,
Gutted cars, earth is calling in her little ones,
"Come home, Come home!" From pig balls,
From the ferocity of pig driven to holiness,
From the furred ear and the full jowl come
The repose of the hung belly, from the purpose
They Lion grow.
                    From the sweet glues of the trotters
Come the sweet kinks of the fist, from the full flower
Of the hams the thorax of caves,
From "Bow Down" come "Rise Up,"
Come they Lion from the reeds of shovels,
The grained arm that pulls the hands,
They Lion grow.
                    From my five arms and all my hands,
From all my white sins forgiven, they feed,
From my car passing under the stars,
They Lion, from my children inherit,
From the oak turned to a wall, they Lion,
From they sack and they belly opened
And all that was hidden burning on the oil-stained earth
They feed they Lion and he comes.

THE CHILDREN'S CRUSADE

Crossbow wanted a child,
a little schoolboy with a red hole
in his brow

like the President. He excited
everyone. They made a brilliant
pair of angel's wings from Kaiser foil

and posterboard, they made a little
tufted box. They would cross his arms
on a single burning peony.

They'd get a glossy Testament,
a blanket tucked in
deep around the sides.

He wanted the little boy who skipped
all the way to school. Eve shook
her red head, and the silver

ignition keys hooked in her
pierced ears chirped. "No, No,"
he was going to be

her lover friend. She wanted
someone like Daddy. Archangel said,
"Daddy."

They took stations.
The night hollered through
the branches and the long grass

like a burned TV.
They bit their hands and waited.
Daddy's car closed.

Everything went quiet and they
had to still their heads like they'd learned
when the bedroom door opened.

After they stabbed him down,
Eve came out from
the shadows. She pulled his beard

but only a little came loose.
She stood so tall in mother's shoes,
and with blue and green chalk

on her lids and cheeks,
he never
knew her. He licked his lips

like when he said important
things, and spread his arms
and made his eyes make tears,

he wanted to talk, he wanted
to help them all, but she just pushed
the knife between his teeth.

When he stopped, they tried
to finish. The box was way too small
and he was too heavy.

So they giggled. When they smelled
what he'd done, they giggled
more. A Daddy going ka ka!

They rolled him over and tore
rags of skin from the eucalyptus
and hid him forever.

Now they ran. The shadows
were all gone, and the air
growing as soft as stone

underwater. Underwater or in moonlight,
the hills rose above the earth,
and they ran shedding their caps and bells,

the little silent bells
they wore at wrist and ankle,
they threw away their names and their no-names.

They cast their knives on the absent waters
and their long bamboo spears.
"Goodbye, rusty can opener, Goodbye!"

The houses were snapping.
It was over and they ran. Never
to wait! Now they were free.

LATER STILL

Two sons are gone.
The end of winter, and the almond blooms
near the back fence. The plum, slower,
unfolds under a streaked sky. The words become,
like prayer, a kind of nonsense
which becomes the thought of our lives.

In middle age we came
to the nine years war, the stars raged
in our horoscopes and the land
turned inwards biting for its heart.

Now in February the pussy willow
furs in the chill wind. In March
the sudden peach, cherry, lilac, in summer
the drumming gourd, corn, grape, and later still
the ghostly milkweed and the last laugh.

TO P.L., 1916–1937

a soldier of the Republic

Gray earth peeping through snow,
you lay for three days
with one side of your face
frozen to the ground. They tied your cheek
with the red and black scarf
of the Anarchists, and bundled you
in canvas, and threw you away.
Before that an old country woman
of the Aragon, spitting on her thumb,
rubbing it against her forefinger,
stole your black Wellingtons,
the gray hunting socks, and the long
slender knife you wore
in a little leather scabbard
riding your right hip. She honed it,
ran her finger down the blade, and laughed,
though she had no meat to cut,
blessing your tight fists
that had fallen side by side
like frozen faces on your hard belly
that was becoming earth. (Years later
she saw the two faces
at table, and turned from the bread
and the steaming oily soup, turned
to the darkness of the open door,
and opened her eyes to darkness
that they might be filled with anything
but those two faces squeezed
in the blue of snow and snow and snow.)
She blessed your feet, still pink,
with hard yellow shields of skin
at heel and toe, and she laughed
scampering across the road, into
the goat field, and up the long hill,
the boots bundled in her skirts,

and the gray hunting socks, and the knife.
For seven weeks she wore the boots
stuffed with rags at toe and heel.
She thought she understood
why you lay down to rest
even in snow, and gave them to a nephew,
and the gray socks too.
The knife is still used, the black handle
almost white, the blade
worn thin since there is meat to cut.
Without laughter she is gone
ten years now,
and on the road to Huesca in spring
there is no one to look for you
among the wild jonquils, the curling
grasses at the road side,
and the blood red poppies, no one
to look on the farthest tip
of wind breathing down from the mountains
and shaking the stunted pines you hid among.

BREATH

Who hears the humming
of rocks at great height,
the long steady drone
of granite holding together,
the strumming of obsidian
to itself? I go among
the stones stooping
and pecking like a
sparrow, imagining
the glacier's final push
resounding still. In
a freezing mountain
stream, my hand opens
scratched and raw and
flutters strangely,
more like an animal
or wild blossom in wind
than any part of me. Great
fields of stone
stretching away under
a slate sky, their single
flower the flower
of my right hand.

      Last night
the fire died into itself
black stick by stick
and the dark came out
of my eyes flooding
everything. I
slept alone and dreamed
of you in an old house
back home among
your country people,
among the dead, not
any living one besides
yourself. I woke
scared by the gasping

of a wild one, scared
by my own breath, and
slowly calmed
remembering your weight
beside me all these
years, and here and
there an eye of stone
gleamed with the warm light
of an absent star.
                    Today
in this high clear room
of the world, I squat
to the life of rocks
jewelled in the stream
or whispering
like shards. What fears
are still held locked
in the veins till the last
fire, and who will calm
us then under a gold sky
that will be all of earth?
Two miles below on the burning
summer plains, you go
about your life one
more day. I give you
almond blossoms
for your hair, your hair
that will be white, I give
the world my worn-out breath
on an old tune, I give
it all I have
and take it back again.

F R O M

1933

ZAYDEE

Why does the sea burn? Why do the hills cry?
My grandfather opens a fresh box
of English Ovals, lights up, and lets the smoke
drift like clouds from his lips.

Where did my father go in my fifth autumn?
In the blind night of Detroit
on the front porch, Grandfather points up
at a constellation shaped like a cock and balls.

A tiny man, at 13 I outgrew his shirts.
I then beheld a closet of stolen suits,
a hive of elevator shoes, crisp hankies,
new bills in the cupboard, old in the wash.

I held the spotted hands that passed over
the breasts of airlines stewardesses,
that moved in the fields like a wind
stirring the long hairs of grain.

Where is the ocean? the flying fish?
the God who speaks from a cloud?
He carries a card table out under the moon
and plays gin rummy and cheats.

He took me up in his arms
when I couldn't walk and carried me
into the grove where the bees sang
and the stream paused forever.

He laughs in the movies, cries in the streets,
the judges in their gowns are monkeys,
the lawyers mice, a cop is a fat hand.
He holds up a strawberry and bites it.

He sings a song of freestone peaches
all in a box,

in the street he sings out Idaho potatoes
California, California oranges.

He sings the months in prison,
sings salt pouring down the sunlight,
shovelling all night in the stove factory
he sings the oven breathing fire.

Where did he go when his autumn came?
He sat before the steering wheel
of the black Packard, he turned the key,
pressed the starter, and he went.

The maples blazed golden and red
a moment and then were still,
the long streets were still and the snow
swirled where I lay down to rest.

GRANDMOTHER IN HEAVEN

Darkness gathering in the branches
of the elm, the car lights going home,

someone's beautiful Polish daughter
with a worn basket of spotted eggs,

an elbow of cabbage, carrots, leaves,
chicken claws scratching the air,

she comes up the cracked walk to the stairway
of shadows and lost dolls and lost breath.

Beautiful Polish daughter with hands
as round and white as buns, daughter

of no lights in the kitchen, no one sits
on the sofa, no one dreams in the tub,

she in her empty room in heaven
unpacking the basket piece by piece

on the silent, enamelled table
with a little word for each, a curse

for the bad back and the black radish
and three quick spits for the pot.

LATE MOON

2 a.m.
December, and still no moon
rising from the river.

My mother
home from the beer garden
stands before the open closet

her hands still burning.
She smooths the fur collar,
the scarf, opens the gloves

crumpled like letters.
Nothing is lost
she says to the darkness, nothing.

The moon finally above the town.
The breathless stacks,
the coal slumps,

the quiet cars
whitened at last.
Her small round hand whitens,

the hand a stranger held
and released
while the Polish music wheezed.

I'm drunk, she says,
and knows she's not. In her chair
undoing brassiere and garters

she sighs
and waits for the need
to move.

The moon descends
in a spasm of silver
tearing the screen door,

the eyes of fire
drown in the still river,
and she's herself.

The little jewels
on cheek and chin
darken and go out,

and in darkness
nothing falls
staining her lap.

AT THE FILLMORE

The music was going on.
The soldier paced outside
his shoes slowly filling

with rain. Morning
would walk early
over the wards of the wounded,

row after row
of small white faces
dragged back.

She dozed in the Ladies
wondering should she
return. This warmth

like the flush of juice
up the pale stem
of the flower, she'd known

before, and its aftermath—
seeing the Sisters
and the promises again.

The music was going on,
a distant pulsing only
from the wilderness of strobes.

He climbed back up
the crowded stairs cloaked
in a halo of rain, and no one

noticed or called.
Nor were those the waters
of the heart she heard

rushing in the booth
beside her. She stubbed
her cigarette and rose.

The music was going on
gathering under
the turning lights, mounting

in the emptying hall
toward the end. They stood
blinded a moment,

and then she offered herself
to his arms and opened
her arms to him, both

of them smiling as they
claimed the other
and whatever else was theirs.

THE POEM CIRCLING
HAMTRAMCK, MICHIGAN, ALL
NIGHT IN SEARCH OF YOU

He hasn't gone to work,
he'll never go back to work.
The wife has gone home, mad,
with the baby on one arm.
Swaying on his good leg,
he calls out to the bare bulb
a name and opens his arms.
The old woman,
the beer gone from her glass,
turns back to the bar.
She's seen them before
with hard, knotted bellies,
with the bare white breasts of boys.
How many times has she stared
into those eyes glistening
with love or pain
and seen nothing
but love or pain.
Deep at night, when she
was coldest, he would always
rise and dress so as not
to miss the first streetcar
burning homeward, and she
would rock alone toward dawn.

If someone would enter now
and take these lovers—for they
are lovers—in his arms
and rock them together
like a mother with a child
in each arm, this man
with so much desire, this woman
with none, then it would not be
Hamtramck, it would not be

this night. They know it
and wait, he staring
into the light, she into
the empty glass. In the darkness
of this world men
pull on heavy canvas gloves,
dip into rubber coats
and enter the fires. The rats
frozen under the conveyors
turn to let their eyes
fill with dawn. A strange star
is born one more time.

LETTERS FOR THE DEAD

The air darkened toward morning
the slag heap's yellow flame
paled against the sky

on the sill the old wren
slept till noon   I wakened
read the paper

and thought of you one by one
and tried to hold your faces
in my eyes

tried to say
something to each of you
of what it is
without you

the winter sun
dipped below the stacks
the chilled tea whitened
in my cup

*

The drug store fired your mother
she dried and hardened

the butcher never returned
to beat his soft palms
against the door

his stiff coveralls hung in the closet
your briefcase
bulged with rusting tools

your shoes aged
the toes curling upward
in a spasm

your voice, your high voice
of pear and honey
shuddered once along the bare walls

but someone ate the pear
someone ate the honey
—we still ate at the usual hours

and went off to the factories in the dark
with bloodless sandwiches
folded in wax paper
with tiny packages of sweets

no one felt your sleep
arriving
or heard the sudden intakes of fear

no one held your hands
to keep them still
or your face glowing like a clock's

at night the toilet ran
a window hummed in the wind
your final letter uncrumpled to the moon

when your father came home at last
drunk repentant eager to beg
there was no one to answer

the salt scattered on the table
untasted

*

On south past Toledo
the bus heading into the great oven
into your first adventure

a man is chewing
a man is lying about love
a frightened corporal loads
and unloads a .45

your face against the black glass
unlined, forever young

out of the miles
of breathing fields suddenly
a small white town
locked against the night
with one light burning

then the cities
the bus hot
and filling with silent
black men

no women anywhere
squad cars hunched on the corners
waiting for life
on past the dark barracks
rail yards
all-night car lots
the last bar winking

At Covington the pale Ohio
inches toward the sea
the bridge gathers its nerves
and you cross
holding your breath the whole way

the dawn of a new world
it grays
climbing the first hills
and up over the grinding ridges

turning slowly to stone
the roadside trees fighting
for light

Later, slate waves
at Pensicola
you stood
and counted them
and turned for home

—The clock silent in the shrunken parlour
the cold plate waiting

*

She dyed her hair black
circled her eyes with blue moons

he drank beer and more beer
till morning splotched his face
his eyes puffed shut

the doctors reworked her face
the mirrors clouded
so she lay with anyone
turning toward the wall
to cry

outside the freezing church
through half the night
his lips soft and pink
as a girl's
he lay down in snow
scratched at trees
tore into his own arms

himself a child
he turned from his children

to shake his fist
in his own face

she married and unmarried
flushed and aborted
she wrote
The jar that stood so high
broke
and fell away
she showed the words to everyone

he whispered into the dead phone
I'm from Dearborn and I'm drunk

They were all we had
of you before the car
shuddered a moment
then faced the coming traffic
all we knew of you
before the siren's pulsing faded
and the white attendant
turned and lit a cigarette

*

3 a.m.
Early April and the house chants
in the night winds
each window gives back
a face
the lie is retold in the heart
the old denials burn
down the hallways of the brain
the dead refuse to die

the air crackles with their angers

the young mother wakens suddenly
and flees her bed and her own children
running over the mountain ground
her old man choking on his lungs
demands to be heard
the aunt paces the closed room
the brother burned in Asia
howls like a tree

And the children die
the sacraments we waited for
go gray
little flat sacks of refuse
and no one can look
or look away

the father, enormous
bunched against the green wall
says
over and over
Can you believe we loved you

All night
rain in the still river
off the loading docks at Wyandotte
locked wheels
blind eyes of cars
the scattered intestines of purses
a pale carp
warped on its side

they bump slowly underwater

*

When will the grass be bread
when will the sea winds bring no salt

to raze the yellow shoots
the pear grind its sand
honey sting the tongue
when will the stars put out their eyes
our hands touch
and the onion laugh

Above Three Rocks
40 miles from here sheep gather
in the mountains
huddling together
in a cup of earth and stone
until a bud of light
flowers in the east
and the old Basque with a cane
comes to lead them down
the passes

*

The sea calmed
the village darkened toward dawn
I was there
awake in a strange room
my children
breathing slowly in the warm air

down the hall
the workers bunched together
three to a bed grunting
in sleep

beside me my wife
in still another world

on the roof
not a single light

the sea reflecting
nothing
one black wave untipped
with spray
slipping toward shore
to spread like oil
—and then no more

nothing moved
no wind
no voice
no sound of anything
not one drop riding down my face
to scald the earth

          *

I ate an apple
the skin the sour white meat
the core
how I relished
the juice
Praise the apple

I struck my strange tall son
again and again
until my wife came begging
from our bed
and pulled me away

for 40 days
I dreamed my death like yours
at great speed
the bones shattering into meat
blood blurring the world
the spirit issuing outward
in a last breath

and came to land
weak and alive
the sunlight crossed my bed
I rose and fed the cat
the green worms fattened
on the vine
I looked in the corners
of things

high on my brother's left shoulder
I carved the old scar
again and again
my signature cut
almost to bone
even the brown silky hairs
and the mottlings from birth
will never hide it

Let the scars shine

south of Cadiz
I stopped the car and ran
in winter mist
to the black margin of the world
the wet rocks stared out unseeing
my tracks crumbled behind me

Bless our blind eyes

*

Early March
a clear and windy day
in the village of Fuengirola
near the new concrete housing project

the workers playing soccer
on their noon break

under a torn roof of rushes
he sat in shadow
legs crossed

a tiny man burned by sun
unshaven for days
a campesino I'd seen
many times coming home
his corduroys dusty
in the first dark
one special Sunday
bearing
a gleaming sea bass
gaffed and dripping
down the length of one leg

a small stiff man
now bowing forward to strike
his forehead against the earth
the left hand flung out
and opened to the sky
the right hand bunched
to his breast

hidden below the cries of play
the words I couldn't understand
the strikings of the earth
again and again
the shakings of the head
NO NO
the eyes riding in tears
seeing and unseeing
the mouth asking everybody and nobody
Why Why

until the trees blackened
the air chilled

111

the oil drums flared
a moment
and died
wind sound only
bamboo creaking through the cold night
and by morning he was gone

tending his patch of lettuce
combing the small field
of fine green onions
stooping all day
to the parched earth

*

No one comes home from school
above the porch
the light takes hold

the papers bleed in a puddle
all night the radio
jives itself

a photo torn in half
dances in the grate
like a cry for help

your books on the shelf
give up their words
one by one

your wedding band
with its secret calligraphy of wear
sleeps in a coffee can

a turnip forgotten
darkens
at the back of the drawer

the mice
settle in the walls
their fierce hearts ticking

Morning—
on the freeway
a white cap skips
and I slow for an instant
and pass

warm days—
the child you never saw
weeds the rhubarb
white grains collect above his lips
and flake away in the sudden wind

even the dead are growing old

GOODBYE

Waking to silence
all the beds empty and made
but mine.
A long autumn morning
the shades drawn past lunch,
the house cool
and quiet, grandmother shushing.
I rode a worn sofa
silently into battle
lashing my flanks.
In the kitchen
uncles and cousins strange
in their serious suits
and shirts, holding
their hands on the table.
The bathroom too warm
and full of smoke, smoke drifting
blue and heavy
in the last cracks of light
long after everyone had gone.

Mama sat
in the living room
in the dark
in the big chair.
She said,
"The good die young"—
not to me or anyone.
It was Mama
with long black gloves
coming out her sleeves
and a black fox
stiffening at her throat.

*

The grass was stiff
and springy, bright green

with yellow and brown spears
burned underneath.
Underneath the willows
I was tired and asked
to lie down in the shade
but had to go right up
to the long dirt hole
red in the sunlight
and say, Goodbye.

Later, beside a still pond
of white ducks
Grandpa sat
and cleaned out my ears
with a white hankie and a match;
he held my face back
in his little speckled hands
and said,
"Your nose is dirty too."

When the woman slid
down on the wet grass
Grandpa took an amber jar
to her nose until she shook
her hair loose
and her eyes rolled open
and she bit her mouth.
The ducks drifted off
under the wooden bridge.
Grandpa said
the baby ducks were
where the children went.

*

In the first light
a sparrow settled outside
my window, and a breeze woke

from the breathing river,
I opened my eyes
and the gauze curtains
were streaming.
"Come here," the sparrow said.
I went. In the alley below
a horse cart piled with bags,
bundles, great tubs of fat,
brass lamps the children broke.
I saw the sheenie-man pissing
into a little paper fire
in the snow, and laughed.
The bird smiled. When I unlatched
the window the bird looked back
three times over each shoulder
then shook his head.
He was never coming back inside,
and rose in a shower
of white dust above
the blazing roofs
and telephone poles.

It meant a child
would have to leave the world.

UNCLE

I remember the forehead born
before Abraham
and flecked with white paint,
the two hands kneading
each other at the sink.
In the basement on Grand
he showed me
his radio,
Manila, Atlantis,
the cities of the burning plains,
the coupons
in comic books, the ads of the air.
Prophet of burned cars
and broken fans, he taught
the toilet the eternal,
argued the Talmud
under his nails. The long boats
with the names of winds
set sail
in the sea of his blind eye.

How could he come
humpbacked
in his crisp undershirt
on the front porch in black Detroit
bringing in the milk,
the newspaper, the bills
long past noon? His truck howls
all night to Benton Harbor, Saginaw,
Dog of the Prairie.
In the high work camps
the men break toward dawn.
He sleeps under a mountain.
Uncle, I call you again Uncle,
I come too late
with a bottle of milk
and a chipped cup of Schnapps

to loosen your fever, undo
your arms and legs
so you can rise
above Belle Isle and the Straits,
your clear eye
rid of our rooms forever,
the glass of fat, the blue flame.

1933

My father entered the kingdom of roots
    his head as still as a stone
    (Laid out in black with a white tie
    he blinked
    and I told no one
    except myself over and over)
    laid out long and gray

The hands that stroked my head
    the voice in the dark asking
    he drove the car all the way to the river
        where the ships burned
    he rang with keys and coins
    he knew the animals and their names
        touched the nose of the horse
        and kicked the German dog away
    he brought Ray Estrada from Mexico in his 16th year
        scolded him like a boy, gave him beer money
        and commanded him to lift and push
    he left in October without his hat
    who answered to the name Father

Father, the world is different in many places
    the old Ford Trimotors are gone to scrap
    the Terraplane turned to snow
    four armies passed over your birthplace
        your house is gone
        all your tall sisters gone
        your fathers
        everyone
    Roosevelt ran again
    you would still be afraid

You would not know me now, I have a son taller than you
    I feel the first night winds catch in the almond

   the plum bend
   and I go in afraid of the death you are
I climb the tree in the vacant lot
   and leave the fruit untasted
I blink the cold winds in from the sea
   walking with Teddy, my little one
   squeezing his hand I feel his death
I find the glacier and wash my face in Arctic dust
I shit handfuls of earth
I stand in the spring river pissing at stars
I see the diamond back at the end of the path
   hissing and rattling
   and will not shoot

The sun is gone, the moon is a slice of hope
   the stars are burned eyes that see
   the wind is the breath of the ocean
   the death of the fish is the allegory
      you slice it open and spill the entrails
      you remove the spine
      the architecture of the breast
      you slap it home
      the oils snap and sizzle.
      you live in the world
   you eat all the unknown deeps
   the great sea oaks rise from the floor
   the bears dip their paws in clear streams
      they hug their great matted coats
      and laugh in the voices of girls
   a man drops slowly like brandy or glue

In the cities of the world
   the streets darken with flies
   all the dead fathers fall out of heaven
      and begin again

the angel of creation is a sparrow in the roadway
storks rise slowly pulling the houses after them
butterflies eat away the eyes of the sun
the last ashes off the fire of the brain
the last leavening of snow
grains of dirt torn from under fingernails and eyes
you drink these

There is the last darkness burning itself to death
    there are nine women come in the dawn with pitchers
    there is my mother
        a dark child in the schoolyard
        miles from anyone
        she has begun to bleed as her mother did
    there is my brother, the first born, the mild one
        his cold breath fogging the bombsight
    there is the other in his LTD
        he talks to the phone, he strokes his thighs
        he dismisses me
    my mother waits for the horsecart to pass
    my mother prays to become fat and wise
        she becomes fat and wise
    the cat dies and it rains
    the dog groans by the side door
    the old hen flies up in a spasm of gold

My woman gets out of bed in the dark and washes her face
    she goes to the kitchen before we waken
    she picks up a skillet, an egg
    the kids go off to school without socks
    in the rain the worms come out to live
    my father opens the telegram under the moon
        Cousin Philip is dead
        my father stands on the porch in his last summer
        he holds back his tears
        he holds back my tears

Once in childhood the stars held still all night
    the moon swelled like a plum but white and silken
    the last train from Chicago howled through the ghetto
    I came downstairs
    my father sat writing in a great black book
    a pile of letters
    a pile of checks
    (he would pay his debts)
    the moon would die
    the stars jelly
    the sea freeze
    I would be a boy in worn shoes splashing through rain

HOLD ME

The table is cleared of my place
and cannot remember. The bed sags
where I turned to death, the earth fills
my first footsteps, the sun drowns my sight.

A woman turns from the basket
of dried white laundry and sees the room
flooding with the rays of my eyes,
the burning of my hair and tongue.

I enter your bedroom, you look up
in the dark from tying your shoes
and see nothing, your boney shoulders
stiffen and hold, your fingers stop.

Was I dust that I should fall?
Was I silence that the cat heard?
Was I anger the jay swallowed?
The black elm choking on leaves?

In May, like this May, long ago
my tiny Russian Grandpa—the bottle king—
cupped a stained hand under my chin
and ran his comb through my golden hair.

Sweat, black shag, horse turds on the wind,
the last wooden cart rattling down
the alleys, the clop of his great gray mare,
green glass flashing in December sun . . .

I am the eye filled with salt,
his child climbing the rain, we are
all the moon, the one planet, the hand
of five stars flung on the night river.

THE NAMES
OF THE LOST

ON THE BIRTH OF GOOD & EVIL DURING THE LONG WINTER OF '28

When the streetcar stalled on Joy Road,
the conductor finished his coffee, puffed
into his overcoat, and went to phone in.
The Hungarian punch press operator wakened
alone, 7000 miles from home, pulled down
his orange cap and set out. If he saw
the winter birds scuffling in the cinders,
if he felt this was the dawn of a new day,
he didn't let on. Where the sidewalks
were unshovelled, he stamped on, raising
his galoshes a little higher with each step.
I came as close as I dared and could hear
only the little gasps as the cold entered
the stained refectory of the breath.
I could see by the way the blue tears squeezed
from the dark of the eyes, by the way
his moustache first dampened and then froze,
that as he turned down Dexter Boulevard,
he considered the hosts of the dead,
and nearest among them, his mother-in-law,
who darkened his table for twenty-seven years
and bruised his wakings. He considered how
before she went off in the winter of '27
she had knitted this cap, knitted so slowly
that Christmas came and went, and now he could
forgive her at last for the twin wool lappets
that closed perfectly on a tiny metal snap
beneath the chin and for making all of it orange.

NO ONE REMEMBERS

A soft wind
off the stones of the dead.
I pass by, stop the car,
and walk among none
of my own, to say
something useless
for them, something
that will calm me under
the same old beaten sky,
something to let me
go on with this day
that began so badly
alone in a motel 10 miles
from where I was born.

I say *Goodbye* finally
because nothing else is here,
because it is Goodbye,
Uncle Joe, big cigar, fist
on the ear, nodding *sure*
bitch and coming at me.
You can't touch me now,
and she's a thousand miles
from here, hell, she may be
dancing long past dawn
across the river
from Philly. It's morning
there too, even in Philly,
it's morning on Lake St. Clair
where we never went fishing,
along the Ohio River, the Detroit,
morning breaking on
the New York Central Express
crashing through the tunnel
and the last gasp of steam
before the entrance into hell
or Baltimore, but it's not

morning where you are, Joe,
unless you come with me.

I'm going to see her today.
She'll cry like always
when you raised your voice
or your fist, she'll
be robed near the window
of the ward when I come in.
No, she won't be dancing.
It's my hand she'll take
in hers and spread on her lap,
it's me she'll feel
slowly finger by finger
like so many threads back
to where the blood died
and our lives met
and went wrong, back
to all she said she'd be,
woman, promise, sigh,
dark hair in the mirror
of a car window all night
on the way back from Georgia.

You think because I
was a boy, I didn't hear,
you think because you had
a pocketful of loose change,
your feet on the desk,
your own phone, a yellow car
on credit, I didn't see
you open your hands
like a prayer and die
into them the way a child
dies into a razor, black hair,
into a tire iron, a chain.
You think I didn't smell

the sweat that rose
from your bed, didn't
know you on the stairs
in the dark, grunting
into a frightened girl.
Because you could push me
aside like a kitchen chair
and hit where you wanted,
you think I was a wren,
a mourning dove
surrendering the nest.

The earth is asleep, Joe,
it's rock, steel, ice,
the earth doesn't care
or forgive. No one remembers
your eyes before they tired,
the way you fought weeping.
No one remembers how much
it cost to drive all night
to Chicago, how much
to sleep all night in a car,
to have it all except
the money. No one remembers
your hand, opened, warm
and sweating on the back
of my neck when you first
picked me up and said
my name, *Philip*, and held
the winter sun up
for me to see outside
the French windows of
the old house on Pingree,
no one remembers.

BELLE ISLE, 1949

We stripped in the first warm spring night
and ran down into the Detroit River
to baptize ourselves in the brine
of car parts, dead fish, stolen bicycles,
melted snow. I remember going under
hand in hand with a Polish highschool girl
I'd never seen before, and the cries
our breath made caught at the same time
on the cold, and rising through the layers
of darkness into the final moonless atmosphere
that was this world, the girl breaking
the surface after me and swimming out
on the starless waters towards the lights
of Jefferson Ave. and the stacks
of the old stove factory unwinking.
Turning at last to see no island at all
but a perfect calm dark as far
as there was sight, and then a light
and another riding low out ahead
to bring us home, ore boats maybe, or smokers
walking alone. Back panting
to the gray coarse beach we didn't dare
fall on, the damp piles of clothes,
and dressing side by side in silence
to go back where we came from.

NEW SEASON

My son and I go walking in the garden.
It is April 12, Friday, 1974.
Teddy points to the slender trunk
of the plum and recalls the digging
last fall through three feet
of hard pan and opens his palms
in the brute light of noon, the heels
glazed with callus, the long fingers
thicker than mine and studded with
silver rings. My mother is 70 today.
He flicks two snails off a leaf
and smashes them underfoot
on the red brick path. Saturday,
my wife stood here, her cheek cut
by a scar of dirt, dirt on her bare
shoulders, on the brown belly,
damp and sour in the creases
of her elbows. She held up a parsnip
squat, misshapen, a tooth pulled
from the earth, and laughed
her great white laugh. Teddy talks
of the wars of the young, Larry V.
and Ricky's brother in the movies,
on Belmont, at McDonald's,
ready to fight for nothing, hard,
redded or on air, "low riders,
grease, what'd you say about my mama!"
Home late, one in the back seat,
his fingers broken, eyes welling
with pain, the eyes and jawbones
swollen and rough. 70 today, the woman
who took my hand and walked me
past the corridor of willows
to the dark pond where the one swan
drifted. I start to tell him
and stop, the story of my 15th spring.
That a sailor had thrown a black baby

off the Belle Isle Bridge was
the first lie we heard, and the city
was at war for real. We would waken
the next morning to find Sherman tanks
at the curb and soldiers camped
on the lawns. Damato said he was
"goin downtown bury a hatchet
in a nigger's head." Women
took coffee and milk to the soldiers
and it was one long block party
till the trucks and tanks loaded up
and stumbled off. No one saw
Damato for a week, and when I did
he was slow, head down, his right arm
blooming in a great white bandage.
He said nothing. On mornings I rise
early, I watch my son in the bathroom,
shirtless, thick-armed and hard,
working with brush and comb
at his full blond head that suddenly
curled like mine and won't
come straight. 7 years passed
before Della Daubien told me
how three white girls from the shop
sat on her on the Woodward streetcar
so the gangs couldn't find her
and pull her off like they did
the black janitor and beat
an eye blind. She would never
forget, she said, and her old face
glows before me in shame
and terror. Tonight, after dinner,
after the long, halting call
to my mother, I'll come out here
to the yard rinsed in moonlight
that blurs it all. She will not
become the small openings

in my brain again through which the wind
rages, though she was the ocean
that ebbed in my blood, the storm clouds
that battered my lungs, though I hide
in the crotch of the orange tree
and weep where the future grows
like a scar, she will not come again
in the brilliant day. My cat Nellie,
15 now, follows me, safe
in the dark from mockingbird
and jay, her fur frost tipped
in the pure air, and together we hear
the wounding of the rose, the willow
on fire—to the dark pond
where the one swan drifted, the woman
is 70 now—the willow is burning,
the rhododendrons shrivel
like paper under water, all
the small secret mouths are feeding
on the green heart of the plum.

ON THE CORNER

Standing on the corner
until Tatum passed
blind as the sea,
heavy, tottering
on the arm of the young
bass player, and they
both talking
Jackie Robinson.
It was cold, late,
and the Flame Show Bar
was crashing
for the night, even
Johnny Ray
calling it quits.
Tatum said, Can't
believe how fast
he is to first. Wait'll
you see Mays
the bass player said.
Women in white furs
spilled out of the bars
and trickled toward
the parking lot. Now
it could rain, coming
straight down. The man
in the brown hat
never turned his head up.
The gutters swirled
their heavy waters,
the streets reflected
the sky, which was
nothing. Tatum
stamped on toward
the Bland Hotel, a wet
newspaper stuck
to his shoe, his mouth

open, his vest
drawn and darkening.
I can't hardly wait, he said.

GIFT FOR A BELIEVER

for Flavio Costantini

It is Friday, a usual day
in Italy, and you wait. Below
the street sleeps at noon.
Once the Phoenicians came that way,
the Roman slaves on foot,
and later the Nazis. To you came
the Anarchists chanting, "We shall inherit,"
and among them Santo Caserio
who lost his head for knifing
the President of France, the ambassador
to hell. Came little Ferrer
in his long gown who taught
the Spanish children to question.
His fine hands chained behind
his back, his eyes of a boy
smeared, he swings above the stone trench
of Montjuich. The wind came
to blow his words away, then snow
that buried your childhood
and all the promises, that rusted
out the old streetcars and humped
over your fathers' graves.
In your vision Durruti whispered
to an old woman that he would
never forget the sons and daughters
who died believing they carried
a new world there in their hearts,
but when the doctor was summoned
and could not stop his wounds
he forgot. Ascaso, who fled
with him to Argentina, Paraguay,
Brussels, the first to die
storming the Atarazanas Barracks,
he forgot. The railyards of León
where his father doubled over

and deafened, forgotten. That world
that he said is growing here
in my heart this minute
forgotten. When old Nathan Pine
gave two hands to a drop-forge
at Chevy, my spit turned to gall
and I swore I'd never forget.
When the years turned to a gray mist
and my sons grew away without faith,
the memory slept, and I bowed
my head so that I might live.
On the spare hillsides west
of here the new lambs stumble
in the fog and rise. My wife kneels
to the cold earth and we have bread.
I see and don't believe. Farther
west the ocean breaks
on cold stones, the great Pacific
that blesses no one breaks
into water. So this is what
I send you, friend, where you wait
above a street that will waken
into dark shops, sellers of flour
and onions, dogs, hawkers
of salt, iron, lies. I send
water to fill your glass
and overflow, to cool your wrists
in the night ahead, water
that runs like a pure thread
through all my dreams
and empties into tears, water
to wash our eyes, our mothers' last wine,
two palm-fulls the sky gave us,
what the roots crave, rain.

WEDNESDAY

I could say the day began
behind the Sierras,
in the orange grove the ladder
that reaches partway
to the stars grew
a shadow, and the fruit
wet with mist put on
its color and glowed
like a globe of fire,
and when I wakened
I was alone and the room
still, the white walls,
the white ceiling, the stained
wood floor held me until
I sat up and reached out
first for a glass
of stale water to free
my tongue, and then
the wristwatch purchased
before you were born,
and while the leaves ticked
against the window and
the dust rose golden
in the chalice of the air
I gave you this name.

MY SON AND I

In a coffee house at 3 a.m.
and he believes
I'm dying. Outside the wind
moves along the streets
of New York City picking up
abandoned scraps of newspapers
and tiny messages of hope
no one hears. He's dressed
in worn corduroy pants
and shirts over shirts,
and his hands are stained
as mine once were
with glue, ink, paint.
A brown stocking cap
hides the thick blond hair
so unlike mine. For forty
minutes he's tried not
to cry. How are his brothers?
I tell him I don't know,
they have grown away
from me. We are Americans
and never touch on this
stunned earth where a boy
sees his life fly past
through a car window. His mother?
She is deaf and works
in the earth for days, hearing
the dirt pray and guiding
the worm to its feasts. Why
do I have to die? Why
do I have to sit before him
no longer his father, only
a man? Because the given
must be taken, because
we hunger before we eat,
because each small spark
must turn to darkness.

As we said when we were kids
and knew the names of everything
. . . just because. I reach
across the table and take
his left hand in mine.
I have no blessing. I can
tell him how I found
the plum blossom before
I was thirty, how once
in a rooming house in Alicante
a man younger than I,
an Argentine I barely understood,
sat by me through the night
while my boy Teddy cried out
for help, and how when he slept
at last, my friend wept
with thanks in the cold light.
I can tell him that his hand
sweating in mine can raise
the Lord God of Stones,
bring down the Republic of Lies,
and hold a spoon. Instead
I say it's late, and he pays
and leads me back
through the empty streets
to the Earl Hotel, where
the room sours with the mould
of old Bibles dumped down
the air-shaft. In my coat
I stand alone in the dark
waiting for something,
a flash of light, a song,
a remembered sweetness
from all the lives I've lost.
Next door the TV babbles
on and on, and I give up
and sway toward the bed
in a last chant before dawn.

A LATE ANSWER

Beyond that stand of firs
was a small clearing
where the woods ran out
of breath or the winds
beat them back. No one
was born there and no one
would be, but you could
bury a lonely man there
or an animal you didn't
want out for flies to eat.
As we passed under the trees
you were cold and took
my hand and felt a shiver
pass through me, but you
didn't let go. When you
spoke at last it was to ask
after my thoughts, but
just then we broke into light
so unexpected I had to close
my eyes and saw the fire
swimming there and had
such a vision of the end
of my life, the trees
turning to great flowers
of flame and the field ringed
with sword bearing angels.
I could say nothing,
but held on to your hand
and you to mine
both in the dream and in
that bare place where
the North Sea winds lashed
our faces with sudden spurts
of rain. Now, on the other side
of the world, years later,
I know the ant came here
believing he would rule

and he waits for the wren
to fall, the grass waits
blowing its breath
into this morning that rises
darkly on wet winds. Somewhere
the sea saves its tears
for the rising tide, somewhere
we'll leave the world weighing
no more than when we came,
and the answer will be
the same, your hand in mine,
mine in yours, in that clearing
where the angels come toward us
without laughter, without tears.

ON THE MURDER OF LIEUTENANT JOSÉ DEL CASTILLO BY THE FALANGIST BRAVO MARTINEZ, JULY 12, 1936

When the Lieutenant of the Guardia de Asalto
heard the automatic go off, he turned
and took the second shot just above
the sternum, the third tore away
the right shoulder of his uniform,
the fourth perforated his cheek. As he
slid out of his comrade's hold
toward the gray cement of the Ramblas
he lost count and knew only
that he would not die and that the blue sky
smudged with clouds was not heaven
for heaven was nowhere and in his eyes
slowly filling with their own light.
The pigeons that spotted the cold floor
of Barcelona rose as he sank below
the waves of silence crashing
on the far shores of his legs, growing
faint and watery. His hands opened
a last time to receive the benedictions
of automobile exhaust and rain
and the rain of soot. His mouth,
that would never again say "I am afraid,"
closed on nothing. The old grandfather
hawking daisies at his stand pressed
a handkerchief against his lips
and turned his eyes away before they held
the eyes of a gunman. The shepherd dogs
on sale howled in their cages
and turned in circles. There is more
to be said, but by someone who has suffered
and died for his sister the earth
and his brothers the beasts and the trees.

The Lieutenant can hear it, the prayer
that comes on the voices of water, today
or yesterday, from Chicago or Valladolid,
and hangs like smoke above this street
he won't walk as a man ever again.

ASK THE ROSES

Snow fell forward forever
I heard the trees counting their breaths
the laughter of the icicle
the rivers turning to stone
What became of the sea's dream
to become spirit and range the sky
what became of the astronomy
of the gopher tunneling under the lettuce
and the onion that died like a saint
from the head down
what became of the wooden heart
of the crow who marked our fields
of two codfish end to end
on a blue plate

In the gay parlours of Barcelona
a widow bought an arm and leg
someone else bought all the names
At sea I buy a cloud
and steer it landward into a pile of cars
I buy a mountain oak
and feed it cocaine until the leaves gag
I read the wolf the oath of office
until he sheds his coat, bites
off his forepaws and howls
for the grave
In front of everyone
I take out my money and count it
stacking the 50's, the 20's, the 10's
The House of Peace, The Mansion of Wisdom,
The Tenement of Beauty
and the Martial Arts, Survival and Torture
We drink to the health of the dollar
Let my people go, say the coins
herded into the black purse
and headed for Germany
No one is going anywhere

we've all come into our own
and we're staying

There are tall reedy weeds by the fence
the fallen oranges in my neighbor's yard
blacken and spread like shotgun wounds
Down south in L.A. they are pouring
milk back to the sewers
Has anyone asked the cows
has anyone told the sunset
it will be on tv or the child
that her breasts filled with plastic
will sell fried chicken
Has anyone told the sea it must count
its tears and explain each one
has anyone told the blood
how long it must crust the sheets
has anyone asked the roses
if they love bees who are
basically communists
and worship the female
has anyone fallen on his knees
and begged the dawn to reconsider
Perhaps it is too late, now
with the golden light of Tarragona
darkening into lead I want to take
a vow of silence, every word
is a young mouse growing in my throat
stretching his paws
trying out his pink nails

As light enters the morning glory
I feel the heart of a tree swell
and grow into mine, as light falls
through the tunnels of branches
that lead back the way I came
I rise from this grave and go

My aunt and my mother sit again
as in the first dreams of home
crying with love for each other
exchanging words they will forget
Later there will be silence
houses will die around them
My aunt will waken in a motel
outside Fort Dix without a name
In the movies my mother will see
the future and run weeping
along the black staircases
studded with huge breathless stars
The old sun will darken like the spots
on her hands, the light will pass early
and she will go on wiping at the air
as at a window, wondering, Is it there
All around her Los Angeles goes on
moaning and blooming, and I wait
for the bus that never comes
or punch the time card
after the clock has stopped

Let the leaves falling singly in my hair
get up and join the tree
let the unread books open
into the nests of barn swallows
or turn to twigs and long grass
yellowing in the summer winds
Let the smell of the egg
mate with the rose and the voice
of elm cry out at dusk, a cat
who will no longer hunt
calling for food, my old cat
full of foolishness and hungers
Shall we dye her blue, call her
"California" and teach her how to turn
how to walk on stage, how to hold

the mouse in her paws
Every evening we show her television
blackening the screen when the lions
drink in the crowded stream

The pen that told the truth melted
on the stove, the ink that held
in its veins the bones
of the eel, let go
They became dirt
metals that are earth and can't fly
or must return to spring water
bitter in a tin cup
A man shelling peas sleeps
under the quarter moon
Anyone who laughs out of turn
must eat flies
At dusk no one dares
if a woman passed me now
she would yell at her dog
snap the leash and try to look old
If she cast her eyes to the ground
I would smell it and shake her head
until her hair caught fire
Smelling myself I think of old clothes
schoolrooms the rain entered and killed
of a leather purse lost at sea
of a mule bleeding along the whipped flanks
a wind passing through a burned hand
the black embers flaking
of air a dog wouldn't breathe
I am space alone, unfilled, waiting day
after day for two people to be together
or only one who could sigh and be still

AND THE TRAINS GO ON

We stood at the back door
of the shop in the night air
while a line of box cars
of soured wheat and pop bottles
uncoupled and was sent creaking
down our spur. Once, when I
unsealed a car and the two
of us strained the door open
with a groan of rust, an old man
stepped out and tipped his hat.
"It's all yours, boys!"
and he went off, stiff-legged,
smelling of straw and shit.
I often wonder whose father
he was and how long he kept
moving until the police
found him, ticketless, sleeping
in a 2nd class waiting room
and tore the cardboard box
out of his hands and beat him
until the ink of his birth smudged
and surrendered its separate vowels.
In the great railyard of Milano
the dog with the white throat
and the soiled muzzle crossed
and recrossed the tracks
"searching for his master,"
said the boy, but his grandfather
said, "No. He was sent by God
to test the Italian railroads."
When I lie down at last to sleep
inside a boxcar of coffins bound
for the villages climbing north
will I waken in a small station
where women have come to claim
what is left of glory? Or will
I sleep until the silver bridge

spanning the Mystic River jabs
me awake, and I am back
in a dirty work shirt that says *Phil*,
24 years old, hungry and lost, on
the run from a war no one can win?
I want to travel one more time
with the wind whipping in
the open door, with you to keep
me company, back the long
tangled road that leads us home.
Through Flat Rock going east
picking up speed, the damp fields
asleep in moonlight. You stand
beside me, breathing the cold
in silence. When you grip
my arm hard and lean way out
and shout out the holy names
of the lost neither of us is scared
and our tears mean nothing.

TO MY GOD IN HIS SICKNESS

A boy is as old as the stars
that will not answer
as old as the last snows
that blacken his hands
though he wakes at 3
and goes to the window
where the crooked fence is blessed
and the long Packard
and the bicycle wheel
though he walk the streets
warm in the halo of his breath
and is blessed over and over
he will waken in the slow dawn
he will call his uncles out
from the sad bars of Irish statesmen
all the old secret reds
who pledge in the park
and raise drinks
and remember Spain

Though he honor the tree
the sierra of snow
the stream that died years ago
though he honor his breakfast
the water in his glass
the bear in his belly
though he honor all crawling
and winged things
the man in his glory
the woman in her salt
though he savor the cup of filth
though he savor Lake Erie
savor the rain burning down
on Gary, Detroit, Wheeling
though my grandmother argues
the first cause of night

and the kitchen cantor mumbles his names
still the grave will sleep

I came this way before
my road ran by your house
crowded with elbows of mist
and pots banging to be filled
my coat was the colors of rain
and six gray sparrows sang
on the branches of my grave

2. A rabbit snared in a fence of pain
    screams and screams
    I waken, a child again
    and answer
    I answer my father
    hauling his stone up the last few breaths
    I answer Moses bumbling before you
    the cat circling three times
    before she stretches out and yawns
    the mole gagged on fresh leaves

    In Folsom, Jaroubi, alone before dawn
    remembers the long legs of a boy
    his own once and now his son's
    Billy Ray holds my hand to his heart
    in the black and white still photograph
    of the exercise yard
    in the long shadows of the rifle towers
    we say goodbye forever
    Later, at dusk the hills
    across the dry riverbed
    hold the last light
    long after it's gone
    and glow like breath

I wake
and it's not a dream
I see the long coast of the continent
writhing in sleep
this America we thought we dreamed
falling away flake by flake
into the sea
and the sea blackening and burning

I see a man curled up, the size of an egg
I see a woman hidden in a carburetor
a child reduced to one word
crushed under an airmail stamp
or a cigarette

Can the hands rebuild the rocks
can the tongue make air or water
can the blood flow back
into the twigs of the child
can the clouds take back their deaths

3. First light of morning
    it is the world again
    the domed hills across the gorge
    take the air slowly
    the day will be hot and long
    Jimmy Ray, Gordon, Jaroubi
    all the prisoners have been awake
    for hours remembering
    I walk through the dense brush
    down to the river
    that descended all night from snow
    small stones worn away
    old words, lost truths
    ground to their essential nonsense
    I lift you in my hand
    and inhale, the odor of light

out of darkness, substance out of air
of blood before it reddens and runs

When I first knew you
I was a friend to the ox and walked
with Absalom and raised my hand
against my hand
and died for want of you
and turned to stone and air and water
the answer to my father's tears

FROM

ASHES

ASHES

THE MIRACLE

A man staring into the fire
sees his dead brother sleeping.

The falling flames go yellow and red
but it is him, unmistakable.

He goes to the phone and calls
his mother. Howard is asleep,

he tells her. Yes, she says,
Howard is asleep. She does not cry.

In her Los Angeles apartment
with its small color tv

humming now unobserved,
she sees Howard rocking

alone beneath the waves
of an ocean she cannot name.

Howard is asleep, she says
to the drapes drawn on the night.

That night she dreams
a house alive with flames, their

old house, and her son sleeping
peacefully in the kingdom of agony.

She wakens near morning,
the dream more real

than the clock luminous beside her
or the gray light rising slowly

above the huddled town, more real
than the groan of the first car.

She calls her son who has risen
for work and tells him,

Howard is warm and at peace.
He sees the crusted snows of March

draining the cold light of a day
already old, he sees himself

unlocking the front door of his shop,
letting the office help in, letting

Eugene and Andy, the grease men
step before him out of the snow.

When she hangs up he looks out
on the back yard, the garbage cans

collapsing like sacks of air, the fence
holding a few gray sparrows,

he looks out on the world he always sees
and thinks, it's a miracle.

STARLIGHT

My father stands in the warm evening
on the porch of my first house.
I am four years old and growing tired.
I see his head among the stars,
the glow of his cigarette, redder
than the summer moon riding
low over the old neighborhood. We
are alone, and he asks me if I am happy.
"Are you happy?" I cannot answer.
I do not really understand the word,
and the voice, my father's voice, is not
his voice, but somehow thick and choked,
a voice I have not heard before, but
heard often since. He bends and passes
a thumb beneath each of my eyes.
The cigarette is gone, but I can smell
the tiredness that hangs on his breath.
He has found nothing, and he smiles
and holds my head with both his hands.
Then he lifts me to his shoulder,
and now I too am there among the stars,
as tall as he. Are you happy? I say.
He nods in answer, Yes! oh yes! oh yes!
And in that new voice he says nothing,
holding my head tight against his head,
his eyes closed up against the starlight,
as though those tiny blinking eyes
of light might find a tall, gaunt child
holding his child against the promises
of autumn, until the boy slept
never to waken in that world again.

NITRATE

They don't come back, he said.
Outside it was dinnertime,
and Granpa's wagon swayed
at the curb, the old gray
shaking his head from side to side
like he wanted to lie down
where the snows had burned off
and dark patches of ground shone.
The house was quiet
so Granpa told me everything
and I understood. They went in
but they never came out.
The hole in the earth
was what they called The Mines,
and that's where his little brother
went in to make his food.
There were horses too
burning up with their carts
like Granpa's bottle cart.
The walls were white as sugar,
soft, and the roots of trees
spun in your face. Granpa wiped
his forehead with the wool cap
and sat staring at the blue smoke
curling from his mouth and said
it was all for a dollar.
He didn't like to cry.
He bowed his head down
and hid his face in his hands,
so he never saw our favorite
Chinese elm out in the front yard,
the green leaves hissing
and steaming like kettles.
A new spring was here
in the last slanting light,
the wren nest went up
in a moment of gold, the eggs

darkening like knuckles.
When the tree was gone
all that was left
was a little mound of salt.

MAKING IT NEW

All morning
rain slowly filled
my hair, misted
my glasses as I broke
the old curbing of US 24,
and Cal, grunting behind,
loaded the pieces
into the wheelbarrow.
"Go slow, man!" but I
was into it. Now, at noon,
we sit under a tree
sharing my lunch. Cal
looks tired, his light
brown skin almost gray.
His father, he tells me,
caught him last night
with white boys in his room.
"I told him, 'Don't look
and you won't see.'" The rain
comes down harder, a wind
picks up, swirling
the few leaves crushed
under the trees. My damp arms
shiver in the sudden chill
of autumn. We are the dignified
by dirt, digging our way
down US 24 to Monroe,
Michigan, where the waters
of Raisin Creek foam
with the milk poured
from the mill, and the great
slow barges from Nineveh
drift in the current,
loaded with yellow spices,
rubies like headlights,
and the whores of the East.
Cal lies back and closes

his eyes. I smoke and let
him sleep. An hour passes
and not one car. At first
his blanket of newspaper
rises in the breeze, a giant
butterfly mottled with slaps
of rain. Cal sleeps on,
his face as open and soft
as a child's, his feet
crossed at the ankles,
the black leather cap
fallen back on the grass.
"Cal," he said the first day,
staring into my eyes,
"is short for Calla, the lily,"
the yellow furled one
his mother so loved. Far off
a car hisses down the road;
it's Teddy, the Captain, come
to tell us it's raining
and we can fly home
or go back to work
or get lost. I leave
Cal, the dark wet bride
of the wind, and go
out into the rain
to get the word—we aren't
ever gonna make Monroe.

ON A DRAWING BY FLAVIO

Above my desk
the Rabbi of Auschwitz
bows his head and prays
for us all, and the earth
which long ago inhaled
his last flames turns
its face toward the light.
Outside the low trees
take the first gray shapes.
At the cost of such
death must I enter
this body again,
this body which is
itself closing on
death? Now the sun
rises above a stunning
valley, and the orchards
thrust their burning
branches into the day.
Do as you please, says
the sun without uttering
a word. But I can't.
I am this hand that
would raise itself
against the earth
and I am the earth too.
I look again and closer
at the Rabbi and at last
see he has my face
that opened its eyes
so many years ago
to death. He has these
long tapering fingers
that long ago reached
for our father's hand
long gone to dirt, these
fingers that hold

hand to forearm,
forearm to hand because
that is all that God
gave us to hold.

ASHES

Far off, from the burned fields
of cotton, smoke rises and scatters
on the last winds of afternoon.
The workers have come in hours ago,
and nothing stirs. The old bus creaked
by full of faces wide-eyed with hunger.
I sat wondering how long the earth
would let the same children die day
after day, let the same women curse
their precious hours, the same men bow
to earn our scraps. I only asked.
And now the answer batters the sky:
with fire there is smoke, and after, ashes.
You can howl your name into the wind
and it will blow it into dust, you
can pledge your single life, the earth
will eat it all, the way you eat
an apple, meat, skin, core, seeds.
Soon the darkness will fall on all
the tired bodies of those who have
torn our living from the silent earth,
and they can sleep and dream of sleep
without end, but before first light
bloodies the sky opening in the east
they will have risen one by one
and dressed in clothes still hot
and damp. Before I waken they are
already bruised by the first hours
of the new sun. The same men
who were never boys, the same women
their faces gone gray with anger,
and the children who will say nothing.
Do you want the earth to be heaven?
Then pray, go down on your knees
as though a king stood before you,
and pray to become all you'll
never be, a drop of sea water,

a small hurtling flame across the sky,
a fine flake of dust that moves
at evening like smoke at great height
above the earth and sees it all.

LOST AND FOUND

A light wind beyond the window,
and the trees swimming
in the golden morning air.
Last night for hours I thought
of a boy lost in a huge city,
a boy in search of someone
lost and not returning. I thought
how long it takes to believe
the simplest facts of our lives—
that certain losses are final,
death is one, childhood another.
It was dark and the house creaked
as though we'd set sail for
a port beyond the darkness.
I must have dozed in my chair
and wakened to see the dim shapes
of orange tree and fig against
a sky turned gray, and a few
doves were moaning from the garden.
The night that seemed so final
had ended, and this dawn becoming
day was changing moment
by moment—for now there
was blue above, and the tall grass
was streaked and blowing, the quail
barked from their hidden nests.
Why give up anything? Someone
is always coming home, turning
a final corner to behold the house
that had grown huge in absence
now dull and shrunken, but the place
where he had come of age, still
dear and like no other. I have
come home from being lost,
home to a name I could accept,
a face that saw all I saw
and broke in a dark room against

a wall that heard all my secrets
and gave nothing back. Now he
is home, the one I searched for.
He is beside me as he always
was, a light spirit that brings
me luck and listens when I speak.
The day is here, and it will last
forever or until the sun fails
and the birds are once again
hidden and moaning, but for now
the lost are found. The sun
has cleared the trees, the wind
risen, and we, father and child
hand in hand, the living and
the dead, are entering the world.

7 YEARS
FROM
SOMEWHERE

I COULD BELIEVE

I could come to believe
almost anything, even
my soul, which is
my unlit cigar, even
the earth that huddled
all these years to
my bones, waiting
for the little of me
it would claim. I
could believe my sons
would grow into
tall lean booted men
driving cattle trucks
to Monday markets,
and my mother would
climb into the stars
hand over hand,
a woman of imagination
and stamina among
the airy spaces
of broken clouds,
and I, middle aged
and heavy, would
buy my suits by
the dozen, vested ones,
and wear a watch chain
stretched across my
middle. Even with none
of that, alone, and
naked at the club,
laid out to be rubbed
down, I would groan
orders to a T-shirted
half-wit. I came
home from Spain, bitter
and wounded, opened
a small portrait shop

in an office building
in Detroit, hired
an alcoholic camera man
and married a homely woman
good with books. It is
1943 and young girls
wait in line for
the white lights blinding
them, drop their blouses
and shoulder straps
and smile for the men
scrambling on Pacific
atolls. I have bought
a second shop
on Washington Blvd.
When I can't stand it
I drive out past the lights
of the small factories
where the bearings for tanks
and half-tracks are ground,
and park and smoke
in silence on the shoulder
of US 24, 7000 miles
from my lost Spain,
a lifetime from the Ebro
where 7 men I came to need
went under in a small boat
and I crossed alone
to a burnt shore and kept
running. Someone said
it was Prospect Park
in the summer, except
for the dying. Except
for the dying this
would be heaven and I,
37 years old, would be
a man I could talk to

or a body fallen away
to the dust of Spain,
a white face becoming
water, a name no one
names, a scramble
of sounds, hiccups
and the striking of teeth
against teeth, except
for the dying I
would be dead, my face
born forever on an
inside page of the Detroit
Free Press, except
for the dying I could
believe.

PLANTING

A soldier runs home
and finds his mother has turned
to iron and the pots are gone.
He finds a small note
from the mice—they took
the silver and won't be back.
How can he return, how
can he march to war
knowing his mother may fall
from the clouds or before that
he may begin to laugh
at nothing and go on laughing
until he grows as tall
as the wayside trees.
He knows he is hungry
and alone. War will do nothing
for him. He knows
each house has gathered
its stories of dust and hurt
and waits under the sycamores
for fire to free it. He knows
it is foolish to be marching
away as long as one cloud
carries the sea back to land.
So he writes a letter
to the year and explains
how he was meant to make
something else, a ball
of earth out of his ears
or music from his wishbone
or a perfect watercolor
from the sparrow's tears, he
was meant to grow small
and still, a window
on the world, a map
that can show him home.
He goes out to the fields

and plants it word by word,
hurling it into the wind
and feels it come back, soft,
burning, heavy with rain.

FRANCISCO, I'LL BRING YOU RED CARNATIONS

Here in the great cemetery
behind the fortress of Barcelona
I have come once more to see
the graves of my fallen.
Two ancient picnickers direct
us down the hill. "Durruti,"
says the man, "I was on
his side." The woman hushes
him. All the way down
this is a city of the dead,
871,251 *difuntos*.
The poor packed in tenements
a dozen high; the rich
in splendid homes or temples.
So nothing has changed
except for the single
unswerving fact: they are
all dead. Here is the Plaza
of San Jaime, here the Rambla
of San Pedro, so every death
still has a mailing address,
but since this is Spain
the mail never comes or
comes too late to be of use.
Between the cemetery and
the Protestant burial ground
we find the three stones
all in a row: Ferrer Guardia,
B. Durruti, F. Ascaso, the names
written with marking pens,
and a few circled A's and tributes
to the FAI and CNT.
For two there are floral
displays, but Ascaso faces
eternity with only a stone.
Maybe as it should be. He was

a stone, a stone and a blade,
the first grinding and sharpening
the other. Half his 36
years were spent in prisons
or on the run, and yet
in that last photograph
taken less than an hour before
he died, he stands in a dark
suit, smoking, a rifle slung
behind his shoulder, and glances
sideways at the camera
half smiling. It is July 20,
1936, and before the darkness
falls a darkness will have
fallen on him. While
the streets are echoing
with victory and revolution,
Francisco Ascaso will take up
the hammered little blade
of his spirit and enter for
the last time the republics
of death. I remember
his words to a frightened
comrade who questioned
the wisdom of attack: "We
have gathered here to die, but we
don't have to die with dogs,
so go." Forty-one years
ago, and now the city stretches
as far as the eye can see,
huge cement columns like nails
pounded into the once green
meadows of the Llobregat.
Your Barcelona is gone,
the old town swallowed
in industrial filth and

the burning mists of gasoline.
Only the police remain, armed
and arrogant, smiling masters
of the boulevards, the police
and your dream of the city
of God, where every man
and every woman gives
and receives the gifts of work
and care, and that dream
goes on in spite of slums,
in spite of death clouds,
the roar of trucks, the harbor
staining the mother sea,
it goes on in spite of all
that mocks it. We have it here
growing in our hearts, as
your comrade said, and when
we give it up with our last
breaths someone will gasp
it home to their lives.
Francisco, stone, knife blade,
single soldier still on
the run down the darkest
street of all, we will be back
across an ocean and a continent
to bring you red carnations,
to celebrate the unbroken
promise of your life that
once was frail and flesh.

MILKWEED

Remember how unimportant
they seemed, growing loosely
in the open fields we crossed
on the way to school. We
would carve wooden swords
and slash at the luscious trunks
until the white milk started
and then flowed. Then we'd
go on to the long day after
day of the History of History
or the tables of numbers and order
as the clock slowly paid
out the moments. The windows
went dark first with rain
and then snow, and then the days,
then the years ran together and not
one mattered more than
another, and not one mattered.

Two days ago I walked
the empty woods, bent over,
crunching through oak leaves,
asking myself questions
without answers. From somewhere
a froth of seeds drifted by touched
with gold in the last light
of a lost day, going with
the wind as they always did.

HEAR ME

I watch the filthy light seep through
the cracked shutters and stain the walls
of this third-rate hotel, and I rise
and go downstairs to walk among
the bodies of the lost men who have
come to die in Barcelona. They are
so small, each a tiny pale planet
whirring slowly toward that burning
each of us will embrace. Open-mouthed
they sigh in the damp morning. Bread
will not save them—holy bread,
common bread, conquered bread, no
bread will save them. Wine they have,
their lips and chins are darkened,
and that didn't save them. If God
cared he would send an old crone
to waken each of them and whisper
that in work is salvation, and
there would be great laughter,
for they have become work.
That one who is still only a boy
is first the ringing of a hammer
on steel. If you put your ear
to his chest you will hear the music
of salvation breaking his heart.
The old one wiping this morning
from his forehead with a soiled cap
was born in a house with a well.
He ate the well, and the four walls,
and the fireless nights that crushed
his hopes. He wants a cigarette.
His work is eating, and before dusk
has climbed the walls of this plaza
he will have eaten the rage
of all our lungs. The others,
why have they come from all
the small places to this place

if not to find the crone hidden
in an English raincoat. The crone
who will not say "conquer your bread"
because I have spit out that lie.
Who will not say, "Take this wine"
because I took it and I am drunk.
Who will not say "work" because I
know that never worked. You,
sitting alone, put your ear
to my chest or take this damp head
motherless from birth and smother
me against the hardened body
of all you've lost, and hear me,
hear me praying to die in Barcelona.

THE LAST STEP

Once I was a small grain
of fire burning on the rim
of day, and I waited in silence
until the dawn released me
and I climbed into the light.
Here, in the brilliant orchard,
the thick-skinned oranges
doze in winter light,
late roses shred the wind,
and blood rains into
the meadows of winter grass.

I thought I would find my father
and hand in hand we would pace off
a child's life, I thought the air,
crystal around us, would hold
his words until they became
me, never to be forgotten.
I thought the rain was far off
under another sky. I thought
that to become a man I
had only to wait, and the years,
gathering slowly, would take me there.

They took me somewhere else.
The twisted fig tree, the almond,
not yet white crowned, the slow
tendrils of grape reaching
into the sky are companions
for a time, but nothing goes
the whole way. Not even the snail
smeared to death on a flat rock
or the tiny sparrow fallen from
the nest and flaring the yellow grass.
The last step, like an entrance,
is alone, in darkness, and without song.

THE FACE

A strange wind off the night.
I have come here to talk
to you at last, here
in an empty hotel room
half the world away from home.
Our tracks have crossed
how many times—a dozen
at least—and yet it's more
than forty years since I saw
you, solemn and hurt, gazing
from your favorite window
at the night that would
soon flood your eyes and darken
the living veins. Below,
the city is almost
asleep. An old man, no
taller than a boy, mumbles
drunkenly on his way,
and then only a sentry
passes from time to time,
his head sunk to his chest,
his eyes closed against
the strange summer cold.

We should all be asleep.
The hour is good for
nothing else, and yet
I cannot sleep because
suddenly today I caught
your presence beside me
on the street as I hadn't
before in all these years.
A tall man laid aside
his paper and stared at me,
a man no older than I,
with the long, sad face

that passed from you
to me. I kept walking,
feeling his eyes on me,
and when I turned at last
he was gone and the bench
filled with dirty children.
I went back—but no—
he was gone, and wherever
I walked I felt those eyes
on me and felt somehow
a time had come when
we might speak at last.

And so I do. I say, Father,
the years have brought
me here, still your son,
they have brought me
to a life I cannot
understand. I'm silent.
A ship is mooring
in the great harbor,
and the only voice
that comes back is the faint
after-ringing of my own.
I say, Father, the dark
moon above this battered city
must once have guided you
across the twelve frontiers
you crossed to save
your life. It leads me
nowhere, for I'm a free man,
alone as you were,
but going nowhere. I too
have lost my three sons
to America, I too have climbed
the long hillsides
of Spain in early light

as our forefathers did,
and gazed down at the sea,
deep and silent. I prayed
for some small hope
which never came. I know
the life you lost. I
have it here, Father,
where you left it, in
the long face of Spain,
in these hands, long
and broken like your own,
in the silence collecting
between each ringing
of my heart, the silence
you anoint me with each day.

Below, the sentry passes
once more in a new light,
for morning is graying
the streets of this quarter.
He wipes his nose on
the rough green wool
of his sleeve and stamps
his feet. Spain will waken
soon to street cries, to
the cries of children,
the cries of the lost men
and women of Barcelona
naming their despair.
I will walk among them,
tired and useless. Today
I will not talk, not
even to myself, for
it is time to listen,
as though some secret
message came blaring
over the megaphones,

or a voice mumbled below
the waves of traffic, as though
one word mattered more
than another in this world,
in this city, broken and stained,
which is the home of no one,
though it shouts out all
our names. I will listen
as though you spoke and told
me all you never knew
of why the earth takes
back all she gives and
even that comes to be enough.

LET ME BEGIN AGAIN

Let me begin again as a speck
of dust caught in the night winds
sweeping out to sea. Let me begin
this time knowing the world is
salt water and dark clouds, the world
is grinding and sighing all night, and dawn
comes slowly and changes nothing. Let
me go back to land after a lifetime
of going nowhere. This time lodged
in the feathers of some scavenging gull
white above the black ship that docks
and broods upon the oily waters of
your harbor. This leaking freighter
has brought a hold full of hayforks
from Spain, great jeroboams of dark
Algerian wine and quill pens that can't
write English. The sailors have stumbled
off toward the bars or the bright houses.
The captain closes his log and falls asleep.
1/10'28. Tonight I shall enter my life
after being at sea for ages, quietly,
in a hospital named for an automobile.
The one child of millions of children
who has flown alone by the stars
above the black wastes of moonless waters
that stretched forever, who has turned
golden in the full sun of a new day.
A tiny wise child who this time will love
his life because it is like no other.

SNOW

Today the snow is drifting
on Belle Isle, and the ducks
are searching for some opening
to the filthy waters of their river.
On Grand River Avenue, which is not
in Venice but in Detroit, Michigan,
the traffic has slowed to a standstill
and yet a sober man has hit a parked car
and swears to the police he was
not guilty. The bright squads of children
on their way to school howl
at the foolishness of the world
they will try not to inherit.
Seen from inside a window,
even a filthy one like those
at Automotive Supply Company, the snow
which has been falling for hours
is more beautiful than even the spring
grass which once unfurled here
before the invention of steel and fire,
for spring grass is what the earth sang
in answer to the new sun, to
melting snow, and the dark rain
of spring nights. But snow is nothing.
It has no melody or form, it
is as though the tears of all
the lost souls rose to heaven
and were finally heard and blessed
with substance and the power of flight
and given their choice chose then
to return to earth, to lay their
great pale cheek against the burning
cheek of earth and say, There, there, child.

WORDS

Another dawn, leaden
and cold. I am up
alone, searching
again for words
that will make
some difference
and finding none,
or rather finding these
who do not
make a difference.
I hear my son
waking for work—
he is late and doesn't
have time for coffee
or *hello*. The door
closes, a motor
turns over, and once
more it's only
me and the gray day.

Lately I've been
running by day,
drinking by night,
as though first to build
a man and then destroy
him—this for
three months, and
I don't find it foolish
—a man almost 50
who still knows so
little of why he's
alive and would turn
away from answers,
turn to the blankness
that follows my nights
or the pounding of
the breath, the sweat

oiling every part
of me, running
even from my hair.

I want to rise above
nothing, not even you.
I want to love women
until the love burns
me alive. I want
to rock God's daughter
until together we
become one wave
of the sea that brought
us into being. I
want your blessing,
whoever you are who
has the power to give
me a name for
whatever I am. I want
you to lead me to
the place within me
where I am every
man and woman, the trees
floating in the cold haze
of January, the small
beasts whose names
I have forgotten, the ache
I feel to be no
longer only myself.

Tonight my son
will come home, his
hands swollen and cracked,
his face gray with
exhaustion. He will
slump before his dinner
and eat. He will say

nothing of how much
it costs to be 18
and tear some small
living for yourself
with only your two hands.
My wife will say nothing
of the helplessness
she feels seeing her
men rocking on
their separate seas.
We are three people
bowing our heads to
all she has given us,
to bread and wine and meat.
The windows have gone
dark, but the room is
quiet in yellow light.
Nothing needs to be said.

YOU CAN HAVE IT

My brother comes home from work
and climbs the stairs to our room.
I can hear the bed groan and his shoes drop
one by one. You can have it, he says.

The moonlight streams in the window
and his unshaven face is whitened
like the face of the moon. He will sleep
long after noon and waken to find me gone.

Thirty years will pass before I remember
that moment when suddenly I knew each man
has one brother who dies when he sleeps
and sleeps when he rises to face this life,

and that together they are only one man
sharing a heart that always labors, hands
yellowed and cracked, a mouth that gasps
for breath and asks, Am I gonna make it?

All night at the ice plant he had fed
the chute its silvery blocks, and then I
stacked cases of orange soda for the children
of Kentucky, one gray boxcar at a time

with always two more waiting. We were twenty
for such a short time and always in
the wrong clothes, crusted with dirt
and sweat. I think now we were never twenty.

In 1948 in the city of Detroit, founded
by de la Mothe Cadillac for the distant purposes
of Henry Ford, no one wakened or died,
no one walked the streets or stoked a furnace,

for there was no such year, and now
that year has fallen off all the old newspapers,

calendars, doctors' appointments, bonds,
wedding certificates, drivers licenses.

The city slept. The snow turned to ice.
The ice to standing pools or rivers
racing in the gutters. Then bright grass rose
between the thousands of cracked squares,

and that grass died. I give you back 1948.
I give you all the years from then
to the coming one. Give me back the moon
with its frail light falling across a face.

Give me back my young brother, hard
and furious, with wide shoulders and a curse
for God and burning eyes that look upon
all creation and say, You can have it.

LET ME BE

When I was first born
the world was another place.
Men were somehow taller
and sang a great deal. I sang
as soon as I could. I sang
to the roads I drove over.
I sang to the winds, and I loved
them. It seems I loved
so much that at times I
shook like a leaf
the moment before it surrenders
the branch and takes the air.
Little wonder I aged so fast,
and before I was forty
I was wizened and tiny, shrunken
like my Grandpa, and like him
afraid of nothing. I think
I would have died early
had I not been reborn
American, blue-eyed, tall.
This time I smoked Luckys,
let my hair grow long,
and never prayed. Except
for the smoking people said
I was like Jesus, except
for that and not knowing
the answers to anything. This
time too I drove badly because
my head was always filled
with tunes and words, and when
the songs went wild, so did I.
Four times I was arrested
for drunk driving, and the police
could not understand a man
so full of joy and empty
of drugs and alcohol. They
would make me walk a line,

but instead I danced and sang
like a lunatic. Yes,
even alone at night, blinded
by their headlights and pushed
by rough unseen hands,
I knew that life was somehow
all I would be given
and it was more than enough.
The months in jail were nothing—
my children came on weekends,
and they seemed proud of me,
though each week I grew
more tiny and tired. They
thought I was happy.
In the soft work shirt and
pale jeans, I was once more
the father of their infancies.
My wife's tears fell burning
my hands, for to her
there was something magical
about me, something that
could not survive the harsh voices,
the bars, the armed men. I died
in her eyes. I could feel
the pain of that death
like a fever coming over me,
rising along my back, up
through my neck and descending
into my eyes like blindness.
This time I died altogether,
without a word, and all
the separate atoms that held
my name scattered into
the mouths of bus conductors
and television repairmen.
I could have lived one
more time as so many

dollars and cents, but given
the choice I asked to remain
nothing. So now I am
a remembered ray of darkness
that catches at the corners
of your sight, a flat calm
in the oceans that never rest,
a yearning that rises
in your throat when you
least expect it, and screams
in a voice no one understands,
Let me be!
Let me be!

7 YEARS FROM SOMEWHERE

The highway ended
and we got out and walked
to where the bridge
had washed out and stared
down at the river moving
but clear to the bottom
of dark rocks. We
wondered, can we go back
and to what? In the hills
of the lower Atlas
7 years ago. You
pointed to a tall shepherd
racing along the crest
of a green hill, and
then there were four,
and they came down, stood
before us, dirty, green
eyed Berbers, their faces
open and laughing. One
took my hand and stroked
the soft white palm
with fingers as brown
and hard as wood. The sun
was beginning to drop
below the peaks, and I
said *Fez*, and they
answered in a language
we hadn't heard before.
Fez, and with gestures
of a man swimming
one told us to double
back, and we would find
a bridge. We left them
standing together in their
long robes, waving and laughing,
and went on to Fez, Meknes,
Tetuan, Ceuta, Spain,

Paris, here. I have
been lost since, wandering
in a bombed-out American
city among strangers
who meant me no harm.
Moving from the bars
to the streets, and coming
home alone to talk
to no one or myself
until the first light
broke the sky and I could
sleep a moment and waken
in the world we made
and will never call
ours, to waken to
the smell of bourbon
and sweat and another day
with no bridge, no old city
cupped carefully in
a bowl of mountains,
no one to take this hand,
the five perfect fingers
of the soul, and hold it
as one holds a blue egg
found in tall grasses
and smile and say something
that means nothing, that
means you are, you
are, and you are home.

ONE FOR THE ROSE

HAVING BEEN ASKED
"WHAT IS A MAN?" I ANSWER

after Keats

My oldest son comes to visit me
in the hospital. He brings giant
peonies and the nurse puts them
in a glass vase, and they sag quietly
on the windowsill where they
seem afraid to gaze out at the city
smoking beneath. He asks when I
will be coming home. I don't know.
He sees there are wires running
from me to a television set on which
my heartbeat is the Sunday Spectacular.
How do I look? I say. He studies
the screen and says, I don't know.
It takes a specialist to tell you how
you look in this place, and none will.
I must have slept, and when I waken
I am alone, and the old man
next to me is gone, and the room
is going dark. This is the Sunday
that will fill the unspoken promise
of all those vanished Sundays
when a shadow on the edge of sight
grew near, enormous, hesitated, and left,
and I sighed with weariness knowing
one more week was here to live.
At last a time and place to die are
given me, and even a small reason.
The flowers have turned now that
the windows have gone dark, and I
see their pale faces in the soft mirror
of the glass. No, they aren't crying,
for this is not the vale of tears.
They are quietly laughing as flowers
always do in the company of men.

"Because this is the place where souls
are made," their laughter whispers.
I will read Keats again, I will rise
and go into the world, unwired and free,
because I am no longer a movie,
I have no beginning, no middle, no end,
no film score underscoring each act,
no costume department, no expert on color.
I am merely a man dressing in the dark
because that is what a man is—
so many mouthfuls of laughter
and so many more, all there can be
behind the sad brown backs of peonies.

THE POEM OF FLIGHT

I shall begin with a rose for courage
and a rich green lawn where the crash occurs
with a sound like an old bridge gasping
under a load, and a white country house
from which a lady and her servants stream
toward the twisted moth. I would be
the original pilot, thirty-one, bareheaded,
my curly brown hair cut short and tinged
with blood from a wounded left hand
that must be attended to. Only an hour
before it was a usual summer morning,
warm and calm, in North Carolina,
and the two hectic brothers had laid aside
their bicycles and were busily assembling
the struts, wires, strings, and cranking
over the tiny engine. I faced the wind,
a cigarette in one hand, a map of creation
in the other. Silently I watch my hand
disappear into the white gauze the lady
turns and turns. I am the first to fly,
and the time has come to say something
to a world that largely crawls, forwards
or backwards, begging for some crust
of bread or earth, enough for a bad life
or a good death. I've returned because
thin as I am there came a moment
when not to seemed foolish and difficult
and because I've not yet tired
of the warm velvet dusks of this country
of firs and mountain oak. And because
high above the valleys and streams
of my land I saw so little of what is here,
only the barest whiff of all I eat each day.
I suppose I must square my shoulders,
lean back, and say something else,
something false, something that even I
won't understand about why some of us

must soar or how we've advanced beyond
the birds or that not having wings
is an illusion that a man with my money
refuses to see. It is hard to face
the truth, this truth or any other,
that climbing exhausts me, and the more
I climb, the higher I get, the less I
want to go on, and the noise is terrible,
I thought the thing would come apart,
and finally there was nothing there.

I WAS BORN IN LUCERNE

Everyone says otherwise. They take me
to a flat on Pingree in Detroit
and say, Up there, the second floor. I say,
No, in a small Italian hotel overlooking
the lake. No doctor, no nurse. Just
a beautiful single woman who preferred
to remain that way and raise me to
the proper height, weight, and level of audacity.
They show me a slip of paper that says,
"Ford Hospital, Dr. Smear, male," and all
the rest of the clichés I could have lived by.
All that afternoon my mother held me close
to her side and watched the slow fog lift
and the water and sky blue all at once,
then darken to a deeper blue that turned
black at last, as I faced the longest night
of my life with tight fists and closed eyes
beside a woman of independence and courage
who sang the peasant songs of her region.
Later she recited the names of small mountain
villages like a litany that would protect
us against the rise of darkness and the fall
of hundreds of desperate men no longer
willing to pull in the fields or the factories
of Torino for a few lire and a Thank You.
She told me of those men, my uncles
and cousins, with names like water pouring
from stone jugs. Primo Grunwald,
Carlo Finzi, Mario Antonio Todesco, Beniamino
Levi, my grandfather. They would die,
she said, as my father had died, because all
of these lands of ours were angered. No one
remembered the simple beauty of a clear dawn
and how snow fell covering the streets
littered with lies. Toward dawn she rose
and watched the light graying the still waters
and held me to the window and bobbed me up

and down until I awakened a moment to
see the golden sun splashed upon the eye
of the world. You wonder why I am
impossible, why I stand in the bus station
in Toledo baying No! No! and hurling
the luggage of strangers every which way,
why I refuse to climb ladders or descend into
cellars of coal dust and dead mice or eat
like a good boy or change my dirty clothes
no matter who complains. Look in my eyes!
They have stared into the burning eyes of earth,
molten metals, the first sun, a woman's face,
they have seen the snow covering it all
and a new day breaking over the mother sea.
I breathed the truth. I was born in Lucerne.

ROOFS

As a child I climbed the roof
and sat alone looking down
at my own back yard, no longer
the same familiar garden.
I thought of flying, of spreading
my arms and pushing off,
but when I did I was back
to earth in no time, but now
with a broken hand that broke
the fall. From this I learned
nothing so profound as Newton
might, but something about
how little truth there was
in fantasy. I had seen that
gesture into air on Saturdays
in the Avalon Theater, where
unfailingly men and women soared
and alighted delicately and with
a calm that suggested they'd
done nothing. My hand bandaged,
I climbed back up and sat
staring over the orderly roofs
to where a steeple rose
or a fire house tolled its bell.
I'd learned something essential
about all that was to come.
The clouds passing over, as I
lay back, were only clouds,
not faces, animals, or portents.
They might carry a real water
that beat fire or knives
and surrendered only to stones,
but no more. The way down
was just like the way up, one
foot following another until
both were firmly on the ground.
Now even a twelve year old

could see he hadn't gone far,
though it was strangely silent
there at the level of high branches,
nothing in sight but blue sky
a little closer and more familiar,
always calling me back as though
I'd found by accident or as in
a dream my only proper element.

THE CONDUCTOR OF NOTHING

If you were to stop and ask me
how long I have been as I am,
a man who hates nothing
and rides old trains for the sake
of riding, I could only answer
with that soft moan I've come
to love. It seems a lifetime I've
been silently crossing and recrossing
this huge land of broken rivers
and fouled lakes, and no one has cared
enough even to ask for a ticket
or question this dingy parody
of a uniform. In the stale,
echoing stations I hunch over a paper
or ply the air with my punch
and soon we are away, pulling out
of that part of a city where the backs
of shops and houses spill out
into the sunlight and the kids
sulk on the stoops or run aimlessly
beneath the viaducts. Then we are
loose, running between grassy slopes
and leaving behind the wounded
wooden rolling stock of another era.
Ahead may be Baltimore, Washington,
darkness, the string of empty cars
rattling and jolting over bad track,
and still farther up ahead the dawn
asleep now in some wet wood far
south of anywhere you've ever been,
where it will waken among the ghostly
shapes of oak and poplar, the ground fog
rising from the small abandoned farms
that once could feed a people. Thus
I come back to life each day
miraculously among the dead,
a sort of moving monument

to what a man can never be—
someone who can say "yes" or "no"
kindly and with a real meaning,
and bending to hear you out, place
a hand upon your shoulder, open
my eyes fully to your eyes, lift
your burden down, and point the way.

THE FOX

I think I must have lived
once before, not as a man or woman
but as a small, quick fox pursued
through fields of grass and grain
by ladies and gentlemen on horseback.
This would explain my nose
and the small dark tufts of hair
that rise from the base of my spine.
It would explain why I am
so seldom invited out to dinner
and when I am I am never
invited back. It would explain
my loathing for those on horseback
in Central Park and how I can
so easily curse them and challenge
the men to fight and why no matter
how big they are or how young
they refuse to dismount,
for at such times, rock in hand,
I must seem demented.
My anger is sudden and total,
for I am a man to whom anger
usually comes slowly, spreading
like a fever along my shoulders
and back and turning my stomach
to a stone, but this fox anger
is lyrical and complete, as I stand
in the pathway shouting and refusing
to budge, feeling the dignity
of the small creature menaced
by the many and larger. Yes,
I must have been that unseen fox
whose breath sears the thick bushes
and whose eyes burn like opals
in the darkness, who humps
and shits gleefully in the horsepath
softened by moonlight and goes on

The Fox

feeling the steady measured beat
of his fox heart like a wordless
delicate song, and the quick forepaws
choosing the way unerringly
and the thick furred body following
while the tail flows upward,
too beautiful a plume for anyone
except a creature who must proclaim
not ever ever ever
to mounted ladies and their gentlemen.

GENIUS

Two old dancing shoes my grandfather
gave the Christian Ladies,
an unpaid water bill, the rear license
of a dog that messed on your lawn,
a tooth I saved for the good fairy
and which is stained with base metals
and plastic filler. With these images
and your black luck and my bad breath
a bright beginner could make a poem
in fourteen rhyming lines about the purity
of first love or the rose's many thorns
or the dew that won't wait long enough
to stand my little gray wren a drink.

TO CIPRIANO, IN THE WIND

Where did your words go,
Cipriano, spoken to me 38 years
ago in the back of Peerless Cleaners,
where raised on a little wooden platform
you bowed to the hissing press
and under the glaring bulb the scars
across your shoulders—"a gift
of my country"—gleamed like old wood.
"*Dignidad*," you said into my boy's
wide eyes, "without is no riches."
And Ferrente, the dapper Sicilian
coatmaker, laughed. What could
a pants presser know of dignity?
That was the winter of '41, it
would take my brother off to war,
where you had come from, it would
bring great snowfalls, graying
in the streets, and the news of death
racing through the halls of my school.
I was growing. Soon I would be
your height, and you'd tell me
eye to eye, "Some day the world
is ours, some day you will see."
And your eyes burned in your fine
white face until I thought you
would burn. That was the winter
of '41, Bataan would fall
to the Japanese and Sam Baghosian
would make the long march
with bayonet wounds in both legs,
and somehow in spite of burning acids
splashed across his chest and the acids
of his own anger rising toward his heart
he would return to us and eat
the stale bread of victory. Cipriano,
do you remember what followed
the worst snow? It rained all night

and in the dawn the streets gleamed,
and within a week wild phlox leaped
in the open fields. I told you
our word for it, "Spring," and you said,
"Spring, spring, it always come after."
Soon the Germans rolled east
into Russia and my cousins died. I
walked alone in the warm spring winds
of evening and said, "Dignity." I said
your words, Cipriano, into the winds.
I said, "Someday this will all be ours."
Come back, Cipriano Mera, step
out of the wind and dressed in the robe
of your pain tell me again that this
world will be ours. Enter my dreams
or my life, Cipriano, come back
out of the wind.

BELIEF

No one believes in the calm
of the North Wind after a time
of rage and depression.
No one believes the sea cares nothing
for the shore or that
the long black volcanic reefs
that rise and fall from sight
each day are the hands
of some forgotten creature
trying to touch the unknowable
heart of water. No one believes
that the lost breath of a man
who died in 1821 is my breath
and that I will live until
I no longer want to, and then
I will write my name
in water, as he did, and pass
this breath to anyone who can
believe that life comes back
again and again without end
and always with the same face—
the face that broke in daylight
before the waves at Depot Bay
curling shoreward over and over
just after dawn as the sky cracked
into long slender fingers of light
and I heard your breath beside me
calm and sweet as you returned
to the dark crowded harbor of sleep.
That man will never return. He ate
the earth and the creatures of the sea
and the air, and so it is time he fed
the small tough patches of grass
that fight for water and air
between the blocks on the long walk
to and from school, it is time
that whatever he said began

first to echo and then fade
in the mind of no one
who listened, and that the bed
that moaned under his weight
be released, and that his shoes curl
upward at last and die, for they too
were only the skins of other animals,
not the bear or tiger he prayed to be
before he knew he too was animal,
but the slow ox that sheds his flesh
so that we might grow to our full height—
the beasts no one yearns to become
as young men dream of the sudden fox
threading his way up the thick hillside
and the old of the full-bellied seal,
whiskered and wisely playful. At the beach
at Castelldefels in 1965 a stout man
in his bare socks stood
above two young women stretched out
and dressed in almost nothing.
In one hand he held his vest,
his shoes, and his suit jacket
and with the other he pointed to those
portions of them he most admired,
and he named them in the formal,
guttural Spanish of the Catalan gentleman.
He went away with specks of fine sand
caught on his socks to remind him
that to enter the fire is to be burned
and that the finger he pointed would
blacken in time and probe the still earth,
root-like, stubborn, and find its life
in darkness. No one believes he
knew all this and dared the sea
to rise that moment and take him
away on a journey without end
or that the bodies of the drowned collect

light from the farthest stars and rise
at night to glow without song.
No one believes that to die
is beautiful, that after the hard pain
of the last unsaid word I am swept
in a calm out from shore
and hang in the silence of millions
for the first time among all my family
and that the magic of water
which has filled me becomes me
and I flow into every crack and crevice
where light can enter. Even my oak
takes me to heart. I shadow the yard
where you come in the evening
to talk while the light rises slowly
skyward, and you shiver a moment
before you go in, not believing
my voice in your ear and that the tall trees
blowing in the wind are sea sounds.
No one believes that tonight is the journey
across dark water to the lost continent
no one named. Do you hear the wind
rising all around you? That comes
only after this certain joy. Do you hear
the waves breaking, even in the darkness,
radiant and full? Close your eyes, close
them and follow us toward the first light.

SOURCES

Fish scales, wet newspapers, unopened cans
of syrupy peaches, smoking tires,
houses that couldn't contain
even a single family without someone
going nuts, raping his own child
or shotgunning his wife. The oily floors
of filling stations where our cars
surrendered their lives and we called
it quits and went on foot to phone
an indifferent brother for help.
No, these are not the elements
of our lives, these are what we left
for our children to puzzle our selves
together so they might come to know
who they are.
              But they won't wait.
This one has borrowed a pickup and a bag
of nails and will spend the light of day
under the California sun singing the songs
the radio lets loose and pounding together
a prefabricated barn. This one lies
back at night before a television set,
a beer in one hand, and waits for
the phone to ring him awake, for
a voice out of the night to tell him
the meaning of the names that fell
together and by which he knows himself.
Out there in the harbor of New York
is Ellis Island, almost empty now
except for the wind that will never leave.
He thinks of the little girl, her name
pinned to her dress, all she is
held in a little bag.
              My distant sons,
my unborn daughters, myself, we
can go on smiling in the face
of the freezing winds that tear down

the Hudson Valley and out to sea, winds
that turn our eyes to white tears, or under
the bland blue sky of this our Western
valley where you sweat until you
cannot hold your own hands. What do we have
today? A morning paper full of lies.
A voice out of nowhere that says, Keep
punching. Darkness that falls each night.
Sea winds that smell of fish scales.
Borrowed cars that won't start and if they did
would go nowhere. Names that mean Lover
of Horses, Hammer, First and Only, Last
but Not Least, Beloved of God. Each other.

RAIN DOWNRIVER

It has been raining now since
long before dawn, and the windows
of the Arab coffee house of Delray
are steamed over and no one looks
in or out. If I were on my way
home from the great chemical plant
on a bus of sodden men, heads rolling
with each swerve or lurch, I would get
off just here by the pale pink temple
and walk slowly the one block back
and swing open the doors on blue smoke
and that blurred language in which two
plus two means the waters of earth
have no end or beginning. I would sit
down at an empty table and open
a newspaper in which the atoms
of each meaningless lie are weighed
and I would order one bitter cup
and formally salute the ceiling,
which is blue like heaven but is
coming down in long bandages
revealing the wounds of the last rain.
In this state, which is not madness
but Michigan, here in the suburbs
of the City of God, rain brings back
the gasoline we blew in the face
of creation and sulphur which will not
soften iron or even yellow rice.
If the Messenger entered now
and called out, You are my people!
the tired waiter would waken and bring
him a coffee and an old newspaper
so that he might read in the wrong words
why the earth gives each of us
a new morning to begin the day
and later brings darkness to hide
what we did with it. Rain in winter

began first in the mind of God
as only the smallest thought,
but as the years passed quietly
into each other leaving only
the charred remains of empty hands
and the one glass that never overflowed
it came closer like the cold breath
of someone who has run through snow
to bring you news of a first birth
or to give you his abrupt, wet blessing
on the forehead. So now I go back
out into it. From a sky I can
no longer see, the fall of evening
glistens around my shoulders that
also glisten, and the world is mine.

THE SUIT

Dark brown pinstripe, the trousers
rising almost to my armpits
and descending, pleated, to great
bellows at the knees, only to close
down just above my shoes. This
was my fine suit, made of God
knows what hard fiber that would
not give or crease. And such
shoulders as no one my height
and under 150 pounds has ever had,
and the great wide swooning lapel
of the double-breasted job buttoning
just below the crotch. So robed, I
was officially dubbed a punk or wild
motherfucker depending on the streets
I glided down. Three times I wore it
formally: first with red suspenders
to a high school dance where no one
danced except the chaperones, in a style
that minimized the fear of gonorrhea.
It was so dark no one recognized me,
and I went home, head down. Then to a party
to which almost no one came and those
who did counted the minutes until
the birthday cake with its armored
frosting was cut and we could flee.
And finally to the draft board where
I stuffed it in a basket with my shoes,
shirt, socks, and underclothes and was
herded naked with the others past doctors
half asleep and determined to find
nothing. That long day it cracked
from indifference or abuse, and so I wore it
on the night shift at Detroit Transmission
where day after day it grew darker and more
unrecognizably tattered like all my
other hopes for a singular life in a rich

world that would be of certain design:
just, proportioned, equal and different
for each of us and satisfying like that flush
of warmth that came with knowing
no one could be more ridiculous than I.

THE VOICE

Small blue flowers like points
of sky were planted to pin
the earth above me, and still
I went on reaching through leaf
and grass blade and the saw-toothed
arms of thistles for the sky
that dozed above my death.
When the first winter came
I slept and wakened in the late March
to hear the flooded fields
singing their hymns to the birds.
The birds returned. And so it was
that I began to learn what changes
I had undergone. Not as in
a sea change had I been pared
down to the white essential
bones, nor did I remain huddled
around the silence after the breath
stormed and collapsed. I was large,
at first a meadow where wild
mustard quivered in warm winds.
Then I slipped effortlessly up
the foothills overlooking
that great awakening valley.
Then it seemed I was neither
the valley below or the peaks above
but a great breathing silence
that turned slowly through darkness
and light, which were the same,
toward darkness and light. I
remember the first time I spoke
in a human voice. I had been
sweeping away the last of sunset
in a small rural town, and I
passed shuddering through a woman
on her solitary way home, her arms
loaded with groceries. She said,

Oh my God! as though she were
lost and frightened, and so I let
the light linger until she found
her door. In truth for a while
I was scared of myself, even
my name scared me, for that's
what I'd been taught, but in
a single round of seasons I saw
no harm could come from me, and now
I embrace whatever pleases me,
and the earth is my one home,
as it always was, the earth
and perhaps some day the sky too
and all the climbing things between.

ON MY OWN

Yes, I only got here on my own.
Nothing miraculous. An old woman
opened her door expecting the milk,
and there I was, seven years old, with
a bulging suitcase of wet cardboard
and my hair plastered down and stiff
in the cold. She didn't say, "Come in,"
she didn't say anything. Her luck
had always been bad, so she stood
to one side and let me pass, trailing
the unmistakable aroma of badger
which she mistook for my underwear,
and so she looked upward, not
to heaven but to the cracked ceiling
her husband had promised to mend,
and she sighed for the first time
in my life that sigh which would tell
me what was for dinner. I found my room
and spread my things on the sagging bed:
the bright ties and candy-striped shirts,
the knife to cut bread, the stuffed weasel
to guard the window, the silver spoon
to turn my tea, the pack of cigarettes
for the life ahead, and at last
the little collection of worn-out books
from which I would choose my only name—
Morgan the Pirate, Jack Dempsey, the Prince
of Wales. I chose Abraham Plain
and went off to school wearing a cap
that said "Ford" in the right script.
The teachers were soft-spoken women
smelling like washed babies and the students
fierce as lost dogs, but they all hushed
in wonder when I named the 400 angels
of death, the planets sighted and unsighted,
the moment at which creation would turn
to burned feathers and blow every which way

in the winds of shock. I sat down
and the room grew quiet and warm. My eyes
asked me to close them. I did, and so
I discovered the beauty of sleep and that
to get ahead I need only say I was there,
and everything would open as the darkness
in my silent head opened onto seascapes
at the other end of the world, waves
breaking into mountains of froth, the sand
running back to become the salt savor
of the infinite. Mrs. Tarbox woke me
for lunch—a tiny container of milk
and chocolate cookies in the shape of Michigan.
Of course I went home at 3:30, with
the bells ringing behind me and four stars
in my notebook and drinking companions
on each arm. If you had been there
in your yellow harness and bright hat
directing traffic you would never
have noticed me—my clothes shabby
and my eyes bright—; to you I'd have been
just an ordinary kid. Sure, now you
know, now it's obvious, what with the light
of the Lord streaming through the nine
windows of my soul and the music of rain
following in my wake and the ordinary air
on fire every blessed day I waken the world.

ONE FOR THE ROSE

Three weeks ago I went back
to the same street corner where
27 years before I took a bus for Akron,
Ohio, but now there was only a blank space
with a few concrete building blocks
scattered among the beer cans
and broken bottles and a view of
the blank backside of an abandoned hotel.
I wondered if Akron was still down there
hidden hundreds of miles south among
the small, shoddy trees of Ohio,
a town so ripe with the smell
of defeat that its citizens lied
about their age, their height, sex,
income, and previous condition
of anything. I spent all of a Saturday
there, disguised in a cashmere suit
stolen from a man twenty pounds
heavier than I, and I never unbuttoned
the jacket. I remember someone
married someone, but only the bride's
father and mother went out
on the linoleum dance floor and leaned
into each other like whipped school kids.
I drank whatever I could find and made
my solitary way back to the terminal
and dozed among the drunks and widows
toward dawn and the first thing north.
What was I doing in Akron, Ohio
waiting for a bus that groaned slowly
between the sickened farms of 1951
and finally entered the smeared air
of hell on US 24 where the Rouge plant
destroys the horizon? I could have been
in Paris at the foot of Gertrude Stein,
I could have been drifting among
the reeds of a clear stream

like the little Moses, to be found
by a princess and named after a conglomerate
or a Jewish hero. Instead I was born
in the wrong year and in the wrong place,
and I made my way so slowly and badly
that I remember every single turn,
and each one smells like an overblown rose,
yellow, American, beautiful, and true.

FROM
SWEET WILL

SALTS AND OILS

In Havana in 1948 I ate fried dog
believing it was Peking duck. Later,
in Tampa I bunked with an insane sailor
who kept a .38 Smith and Wesson in his shorts.
In the same room were twins, oilers
from Toledo, who argued for hours
each night whose turn it was
to get breakfast and should he turn
the eggs or not. On the way north
I lived for three days on warm water
in a DC-6 with a burned out radio
on the runway at Athens, Georgia. We sang
a song, "Georgia's Big Behind," and prayed
for WWIII and complete, unconditional surrender.
Napping in an open field near Newport News,
I chewed on grass while the shadows of September
lengthened; in the distance a man hammered
on the roof of a hangar and groaned how he
was out of luck and vittles. Bummed a ride
in from Mitchell Field and had beet borscht
and white bread at 34th and 8th Avenue.
I threw up in the alley behind the YMCA
and slept until they turned me out.
I walked the bridge to Brooklyn
while the East River browned below.
A mile from Ebbetts Field, from all
that history, I found Murray, my papa's
buddy, in his greasy truck shop, polishing
replacement parts. Short, unshaven, puffed,
he strutted the filthy aisles,
a tiny Ghengis Khan. He sent out for soup
and sandwiches. The world turned on barley,
pickled meats, yellow mustard, kasha,
rye breads. It rained in October, rained
so hard I couldn't walk and smoke, so I
chewed pepsin chewing gum. The rain
spoiled Armistice Day in Lancaster, Pa.

The open cars overflowed, girls cried,
the tubas and trombones went dumb,
the floral displays shredded, the gutters
clogged with petals. Afterwards had ham
on buttered whole-wheat bread, ham
and butter for the first time
on the same day in Zanesville with snow
forecast, snow, high winds, closed roads,
solid darkness before 5 p.m. These were not
the labors of Hercules, these were not
of meat or moment to anyone but me
or destined for story or to learn from
or to make me fit to take the hand
of a toad or a toad princess or to stand
in line for food stamps. One quiet morning
at the end of my thirteenth year a little bird
with a dark head and tattered tail feathers
had come to the bedroom window and commanded
me to pass through the winding miles
of narrow dark corridors and passageways
of my growing body the filth and glory
of the palatable world. Since then I've
been going out and coming back
the way a swallow does with unerring grace
and foreknowledge because all of this
was prophesied in the final, unread book
of the Midrash and because I have to
grow up and because it pleases me.

THE WHITE IRIS

A single stalk climbed up
to my window to hold out
its long white bud. Late March
under a slow sky, the alder
shudders in the west wind
and stills, even the jays
have quieted.
                    Yesterday
just after dawn, I found
my tall son John working
the garden paths. Unable
to sleep he had come home
on foot through the dark town
to take up the shovel
and the hoe.
                    Now the rain
dances on the shed roof, bows
down the wild asparagus,
and blackens the earth. If I
wakened in the stillness
of this afternoon, I'd find
a blue sky and the iris
beaten open into blossom.

LOOK

The low-built houses of the poor
were all around him, and it
was dawn now, and he was more
awake than not. So it is
a young man begins his life.
Someone, probably his brother,
has quietly closed the front
door, and he feels a sudden gust
of cold air and opens his eyes.
Through the uncurtained window
the great factory sulks in gray
light, there where his mother
must be finishing the night,
her arms crossed and immersed
in the deep, milky washbasin,
those long and slender arms
that seem to him as hard
and drawn as a man's, and
now she would be smiling
with one eye closed and blurred
by the first cigarette in hours.
He sits up and lights his first
too and draws the smoke in
as deeply as he can and feels
his long nakedness stretched
out before him, filling the bed
now grown too small for him.
They will pass, mother and son,
on the street, and he will hold
her straight, taut body for
a moment and smell the grease
in her hair and touch her lips
with his, and today he will not
wonder why the tears start and
stall in her eyes and in his.
Today for the first time in
his life he will let his hands

stray across her padded back
and shoulders, feeling them
give and then hold, and he will
not say one word, not *mother*
or *Ruth* or *goodbye*. If you
are awake in the poor light
of this November, have a look
down at the street that leads
the way you too will have soon
to take. Do you see them there
stopped in each others' arms,
these two who love each other?
Go ahead and look! You wanted
to live as much as they did,
you asked the day to start,
and the day started, but not
because you asked. Forward
or back, they've got no place
to go. No one's blaming you.

SWEET WILL

The man who stood beside me
34 years ago this night fell
on to the concrete, oily floor
of Detroit Transmission, and we
stepped carefully over him until
he wakened and went back to his press.

It was Friday night, and the others
told me that every Friday he drank
more than he could hold and fell
and he wasn't any dumber for it
so just let him get up at his
own sweet will or he'll hit you.

"At his own sweet will," was just
what the old black man said to me,
and he smiled the smile of one
who is still surprised that dawn
graying the cracked and broken windows
could start us all to singing in the cold.

Stash rose and wiped the back of his head
with a crumpled handkerchief and looked
at his own blood as though it were
dirt and puzzled as to how
it got there and then wiped the ends
of his fingers carefully one at a time

the way the mother wipes the fingers
of a sleeping child, and climbed back
on his wooden soda-pop case to
his punch press and hollered at all
of us over the oceanic roar of work,
addressing us by our names and nations—

"Nigger, Kike, Hunky, River Rat,"
but he gave it a tune, an old tune,
like "America the Beautiful." And he danced
a little two-step and smiled showing
the four stained teeth left in the front
and took another suck of cherry brandy.

In truth it was no longer Friday,
for night had turned to day as it
often does for those who are patient,
so it was Saturday in the year of '48
in the very heart of the city of man
where your Cadillac cars get manufactured.

In truth all those people are dead,
they have gone up to heaven singing
"Time on My Hands" or "Begin the Beguine,"
and the Cadillacs have all gone back
to earth, and nothing that we made
that night is worth more than me.

And in truth I'm not worth a thing
what with my feet and my two bad eyes
and my one long nose and my breath
of old lies and my sad tales of men
who let the earth break them back,
each one, to dirty blood or bloody dirt.

Not worth a thing! Just like it was said
at my magic birth when the stars
collided and fire fell from great space
into great space, and people rose one
by one from cold beds to tend a world
that runs on and on at its own sweet will.

FROM A POEM WITH NO ENDING

The memory of rain falling slowly
into the dark streets and the smell
of a new season rising above
the trucks parked in silent rows.
Even without earth or snow melting
or new grass rising into moonlight,
the year is turning, and the streets
can feel it. I dreamed this,
or I lived it for a moment, waking
in the night to no bird song
or wind pull, waking to no one
beside me asking for water
or a child calling from another room.
Awake now for a second or a lifetime,
I'm once again stepping out onto
the tiny veranda above the railyards
of Sevilla. In the room next door
a soldier has dressed a chair
with his uniform and leaned his rifle
against the glass door. A woman's clothes
are scattered on the floor. I look away.
Christmas, 1965. The halls of this hotel
are filled with sleeping peasants.
Each of my three sons is alone
in a narrow room with no windows,
asleep in a darkness beyond darkness,
and I feel their loneliness and fear.
Below the window, the lights
of the railyard flash this way
and that, and an old engine is firing up.
Distant voices speak out, but I can't
understand their words. I am falling
toward sleep again. For a moment
I feel my arms spread wide to enclose
everyone within these walls whitewashed
over and over, my own sons, my woman,
and all the other sons and daughters

stretched out or curled up in bad beds
or on bare floors, their heads
pillowed on their own hard arms,
their cheeks darkened by cheap newsprint.
There is a song, bird song or wind song,
or the song old rooms sing when no one
is awake to hear. For a moment I
almost catch the melody we make
with bare walls, old iron sagging beds,
and scarred floors. There is one
deep full note for each of us.
This is the first night of my life
I know we are music.

*

                       Across the world
in the high mountains of the West,
I had gone one Sunday
with my youngest son, Teddy.
We parked the car and climbed
from the road's end over a rise
of young pines and then descended
slowly for a mile or more
through a meadow of wildflowers
still blooming in July. The yellow
ones that reached to his shoulders
stained my legs with pollen.
As we walked he spoke of animals
with the gift of speech. Bears,
he told me, were especially fond
of young people, and the mother bears
were known for coming into towns
like ours to steal boys and girls
and bring them back up here and teach
them hunting, and the children
grew into animals and forgot

245

their homes and their brothers.
A slight rise, and we entered
a thick forest. The air was still
and damp, and there was no longer
any trail. Soon I lost my way.
In a small clearing we stopped
to have our sandwiches, and I cooled
the soda pop in a stream whose rushing
we'd heard from far off. His head
pillowed on his jacket, he lay out,
eyes closed, the long dark lashes
quivering in sunlight, the cheeks
brown and smooth. When I awoke
he was throwing rocks as large
as he could manage into the stream
where they banged down a stairway
of stone and came to rest. The sun
had shifted, the shadows fell
across our faces, and it was cooler.
He was building a house, he said,
below the water, dark now, and boiling.
I bet him he couldn't lead us back
the way we'd come through the dark
bear woods and across the great plain
and up and down these hills.
A dollar? he said. Yes. And talking
all the way, he took the lead,
switching a fallen branch before him
to dub this little tree as friend
or a tall weed as enemy, stopping once
to uproot a purple wildflower for me.

*

I reenter a day in a late summer,
the heat going from the streets
and the cramped downriver flats, a day

of departures and farewells, for I
too am going, packing my box
of books and my typewriter and heading
West this time. So it seems
that all of us are on the move,
giving up these jobs that gave us
just enough and took all we had.
Going back to the little hollows
we'd come away from when the land
gave out or going back
to the survivors left in Alabama
or farther back to the villages
of Greece and Italy. From all
of these people I take a drink,
a pastry, and a coin to insure
a safe voyage, and we shake hands
around the battered kitchen tables.
Sometimes the old ones turn away
before I leave and cry without sound
or sometimes a man touches
his wife, but more often each stands
alone and silent in the old pain.

*

How many lives were torn apart
in those years? How many young men
went off as ours did but never
came back? It was still dark when we
drove into the great harbor and found
the ship to Sweden and said goodbye
not knowing what it was we said.
We saw him climb the gangplank
loaded down with duffle bags
and a guitar he scarcely played.
We turned back to the city
unable to face each other,

unable to face the coming day.
The sun shone on trams and markets,
and until late afternoon I tramped
the streets no longer looking for
the face I sought in childhood,
for now that face was mine, and I
was old enough to know
that my son would not suddenly
turn a corner and be mine
as I was my father's son.
A woman came out of a bar
screaming at her man, and he
hurried silently beside me
and darted quickly down an alley.
When I turned the woman's face
was smeared with tears. She shook
a finger at me and damned me
in her tongue. That night I
slept alone and dreamed of finding
my way back to the house where I
was born. It was quiet when I
entered, for no one had risen yet,
and I climbed the steps to my room
where nothing stirred in all
the rooms beneath me. I slept
fully dressed, stretched out
on a tiny bed, a boy's bed,
and in that dream more vivid
than the waking from it, the rooms
were one and I was home at last.

*

To get west you go east.
You leave in the dark
by car and drive until you
can't and sleep by the road

for an hour or a moment.
If the windshield is crystalled
when you waken you know
the days will be getting
colder and shorter. If you
wake soaked with sweat
then the year is turning
toward summer. None of
it matters at all, the towns
you travel through, plunging
down hills and over the cobbles
and the twisting tight passageways
and breaking for the open fields,
the apple orchards and the barns
rotting and fallen, none of it
matters to you. No one
you know dreams these houses
or hides here from the rain.
When the long day turns
to dark and you're nowhere
you've ever been before, you
keep going, and the magic eyes
that gleam by the roadside
are those of animals come
down from the invisible hills.
Yes, they have something to tell
or something to give you
from a world you've lost.
If you stopped the car and let
the engine idle and walked
slowly toward them, one hand
held out in greeting, you
would find only a fence post
bullet-scarred and deckled with
red-eyed reflectors. None
of it matters, so just keep going,
forward or back, until you've

found the place or the place
doesn't matter. They were only
animals come down to stand
in silent formation by a road
you traveled.

*

We sat by the shore
together as the sea rose in sharp
waves and turned a darker blue.
The families around us shook out
their blankets and gathered up
what remained of their meals
under the sun. A sea wind blew
in and tore their words away and set
the sand to twisting about us.
When my eyes stopped watering
sky and sea were one black cloth
broken by no light, and we walked
back to the little unlighted station
where the dark-eyed children dozed
on benches beside their mothers.
The cars were crowded. The train
stopped at each sea town to pick up
the last stragglers, and we stood
pressed together, groaning, as we
jarred and jolted over the old track
and finally entered the black tunnel
that led to the center of the city.
In the plaza young couples whispered
together and soldiers passed in pairs,
armed and silent, their faces
glistening between the heavy wool
of cap and tunic. We walked the long
avenue back to our room, back to
the empty crippled bed that held

a place for us. Now this is home,
I thought, now I live nowhere
and have made friends with the seas
that work even while I sleep. I
see in the ocean of my memory
the shore birds going out and nothing
coming back. No light enters
the little room, but I can hear
the unsteady tapping of an old man
going home and the young starting
out for work. It's Monday morning
now, and their harsh voices rise
calling out to each other or
to no one in cries or in songs
that fill my sleep. I see beyond
the dark the distant sky breaking
into color and each wave taking
shape and rising landward.

AN ORDINARY MORNING

A man is singing on the bus
coming in from Toledo.
His voice floats over the heads
that bow and sway with each
turn, jolt, and sudden slowing.
A hoarse, quiet voice, it tells
of love that is true, of love
that endures a whole weekend.
The driver answers in a tenor
frayed from cigarettes, coffee,
and original curses thrown
down from his seat of command.
He answers that he has time
on his hands and it's heavy.
O heavy hangs the head, he
improvises, and the man
back in the very last row,
bouncing now on the cobbles
as we bump down the boulevard,
affirms that it is hanging,
yes, and that it is heavy.
This is what I waken to.
One by one my near neighbors
open their watering eyes
and close their mouths to accept
this bright, sung conversation
on the theme of their morning.
The sun enters from a cloud
and shatters the wide windshield
into seventeen distinct shades
of yellow and fire, the brakes
gasp and take hold, and we are
the living, newly arrived
in Detroit, city of dreams,
each on his own black throne.

JEWISH GRAVEYARDS, ITALY

dust

Within a low wall falling away
into dust, a few acres of stones,
wildflowers, tall grasses, weeds.
By the house, firewood stacked
neatly for the winter ahead. Now
it is summer, and even before noon
the heat is rising to stun us all,
the crickets, salamanders, ants.
The large, swart flies circle slowly
in air around something I can't see
and won't be waved away. The old man
who answered the bell and let me in
has gone back to his rocking chair
and sits bareheaded softly whistling
a song I've forgotten. Dove moans,
or something like them, from under
the low, scorched pines, and farther
off the laughter of other birds,
and beyond the birds, the hum
of a distant world still there.
A truck gearing down to enter town,
an auto horn, perhaps the voices
of children leaving school, for it's
almost that time. A low wind
raises the hankie I've knotted
at the corners, and with one hand
I hold it and bend to the names
and say them as slowly as I can.
Full, majestic, vanished names
that fill my mouth and go out
into the densely yellowed air
of this great valley and dissolve
as even the sea dissolves beating
on a stone shore or as love does
when the beloved turns to stone

or dust or water. The old man
rocks and whistles by turns
into the long afternoon, and I
bow again to what I don't know.

shade

Wild roses bursting
in the branches of low hemlocks, thistles
to which the bees swarm.
I've come out of the heat of the city to rest
in the shade of death,
but at noon there's no more shade in this place
than on the streets.
As for death, I saw only a huge symbolic spider
that refused to scuttle
into a bin of firewood when I snapped my hankie.
The wood was green olive,
the twisting branches stacked in two-foot lengths.
Once upon a time
when even the weather proved too much, I would
close my eyes and find
another weather. The raw azures and corals
of the soul raged across
the great, black pastures of my childhood
at their pleasure.
That was prayer. But now when I open them
I don't find the grave
of the unknown English poet the world scorned
or his friend who lived,
I don't hear the music of a farther life beyond
this life. I hear traffic
not far off. I see small wild daisies climbing
the weeds that sprout
from the grave of Sofia Finzi Hersch, who died
in New Jersey and rests

among her Italian relatives. I feel my legs
cramp in this odd posture,
for I'm kneeling. I feel the cold damp of soil
given back to the earth
before the earth could take it back, and the heat
familiar on my back
bowed in the poor shade of a rusting alder.

rain

At the end of a street of rain
there's always a place to find,
a gray rope to pull, a dull ringing
from within, an old frowning woman
shuffling in felt house slippers
to unlock the gate and say nothing.
A rusted barrow in an alcove,
shovels crossed on mounded dirt,
then the sad acres of polished stones
fallen this way and that. I can
stand under an umbrella, a man
in a romance I never finished
come to tell the rain a secret
the living don't want and the dead know:
how life goes on, how seasons pass,
the children grow, and the earth gives
back what it took. My shoes darken.
I move from one cluster of stones
to another studying the names
and dates that tell me nothing I
hadn't guessed. In sunlight, in moonlight,
or in rain, it's always the same,
whatever truth falls from the sky
as slowly as dust settling in
morning light or cold mist rising
from a river, takes the shape

I give it, and I can't give it any.
A wind will come up if I stand
here long enough and blow the clouds
into smoking shapes of water
and earth. Before the last darkness
rises from the wet wild grasses,
new soft rays of late sunlight
will fall through, promising nothing.
They overflow the luminous thorns
of the roses, they catch fire
for a moment on the young leaves.

A WALK WITH
TOM JEFFERSON

BUYING AND SELLING

All the way across the Bay Bridge I sang
to the cool winds buffeting my Ford,
for I was on my way to a life of buying
untouched drive shafts, universal joints,
perfect bearings so steeped in Cosmoline
they could endure a century and still retain
their purity of functional design, they
could outlast everything until like us
their usefulness became legend and they
were transformed into sculpture. At Benicia
or the Oakland Naval Yard or Alameda
I left the brilliant Western sun behind
to enter the wilderness of warehouses
with one sullen enlisted man as guide.
There under the blinking artificial light
I was allowed to unwrap a single sample,
to hack or saw my way with delicacy
through layer after layer of cardboard,
metallic paper, cloth webbing, wax
as hard as wood until the dulled steel
was revealed beneath. I read, if I could,
the maker's name, letters, numbers,
all of which translated into functions
and values known only to the old moguls
of the great international junk companies
of Chicago, Philadelphia, Brooklyn,
whose young emissary I was. I, who at
twenty had wept publicly in the Dexter-
Davison branch of the public library
over the death of Keats in the Colvin
biography and had prayed like him
to be among the immortals, now lived
at thirty by a code of figures so arcane
they passed from one side of the brain
to the other only in darkness. I, who
at twenty-six had abandoned several careers
in salesmanship— copper kitchenware,

259

Fuller brushes, American encyclopedias—
from door to unanswered door in the down
and out neighborhoods of Detroit, turning
in my sample cases like a general handing
over his side arms and swagger stick, I
now relayed the new gospels across mountains
and the Great Plains states to my waiting masters.
The news came back: Bid! And we did
and did so in secret. The bids were
awarded, so trucks were dispatched,
Mohawks, Tam O'Shanters, Iroquois.
In new Wellingtons, I stood to one side
while the fork lifts did their work,
entering only at the final moment to pay
both loaders and drivers their pittances
not to steal, to buy at last what could
not be bought. The day was closing down.
Even in California the afternoon skies
must turn from blue to a darker blue
and finally take the color of coal, and stars
—the same or similar ones—hidden so long
above the Chicago River or the IRT
to Brooklyn, emerge stubbornly not in ones
but in pairs, for there is safety in numbers.
Silent, alone, I would stand in the truck's
gray wake feeling something had passed,
was over, complete. The great metal doors
of the loading dock crashed down, and in
the sudden aftermath I inhaled a sadness
stronger than my Lucky Strike, stronger
than the sadness of these hills and valleys
with their secret ponds and streams unknown
even to children, or the sadness of children
themselves, who having been abandoned believe
their parents will return before dark.

MAKING LIGHT OF IT

I call out a secret name, the name
of the angel who guards my sleep,
and light grows in the east, a new light
like no other, as soft as the petals
of the blown rose of late summer.
Yes, it is late summer in the West.
Even the grasses climbing the Sierras
reach for the next outcropping of rock
with tough, burned fingers. The thistle
sheds its royal robes and quivers
awake in the hot winds off the sun.
A cloudless sky fills my room, the room
I was born in and where my father sleeps
his long dark sleep guarding the name
he shared with me. I can follow the day
to the black rags and corners it will
scatter to because someone always
goes ahead burning the little candle
of his breath, making light of it all.

WINTER WORDS

For Tu Fu

Day after day in a high room between
two rivers, I sit alone and welcome
morning across the junked roof tops
of Harlem. Fifteen stories up, neither
on a cloud of soot nor a roof of stone,
I am in my element, urging the past
out of its pockets of silence.
                    The friends
of my first poems long banished
into silence and no time, leaving nothing
to tell me who they are.
                   A nail of sunlight
on the George Washington Bridge. The first cars
crossing to the island douse their lights
and keep coming. They'll be joining us,
these early risers from New Jersey.

*

Sheets of rain falling in the descending
evening dark. Red lights of the chicken shack
at Manhattan and 125th. The bridge lights,
green and white. A siren comes on yelping,
and another. The rain doubles and smears
the night across the wide world.
                    Years ago
by the mudflats of the Llobregat
we walked in the late mist. Wild bird cry
from a shivering stand of bamboo.
The high voices of young women and girls
as they gathered the long day's remnants.
In the half-dark a child found three feathers
of a kingfisher and took them as a gift
of nature and gave me one.
                I hold it
now on my open palm for a moment.

It rises slowly and settles on no wind
but my breathing, the colors softened
to the usual shades of rain, night, sleep.

*

From where I stand the Hudson barely moves—
over an hour and nothing has passed
up or down. I can see a few tugs smoking
on the Jersey side, and when the sky lifts
gray daylight falls on barges, warehouses,
rail yards, black mountains of tenements,
the smoking stacks of factories.
                         Once I slept
beside a wide river whose currents pulled
both night and day. I thought it began
at the source of all sweet waters and took them
through seven small seas to a great ocean
tasting of salt and our lives.
                         When the sun breaks
through the full clouds of boyhood, we are there
waiting on the dock in our summer suits
for bright lake boats with the names of islands.

*

Birthday tulips, twelve hothouse flowers
of royal purple on long stilt-like legs
that sag beside the frosted window.
Paper white narcissus uncoiled from bulbs
that had only polished stones to push
their green shoots through. You can grow up here.

East I can see to Throg's Neck, a pale bridge
that leads to Connecticut, and above
the bridge a skyway of air the birds
could take if they wanted another world.

263

Down below in an empty parking lot
I find my favorite, the sparrow
who picks about the gravel, and he invites
me in with a twist of his head, a knock
of his beak. You can grow down here.

*

Snow flakes racing across my window,
then wind-checked, reversed, wheeling
back east to west.
               At Puigcerda
on the way back from the holy valley
of Andorra, clouds of black starlings
rising at dusk from bare winter trees
and the hard ashen fields of December,
a twisting cloud above the road. They knew
where they were going.
                   Still more snow until
slowly the dark rooftops below erase
their sullen faces. One lost seagull
against a featureless gray sky,
white wings extended, hung
motionless above the changing winds.

*

Above the bridge lights a rope of stars.
Alone, late at night, my breath fogging
the window, I can almost believe
the sleeping world is the reflection
of heaven.
            Detroit, 1951,
Friday night, after swing shift we drove
the narrow, unmarked country roads searching
for Lake Erie's Canadian shore.
Later, wrapped in rough blankets, barefoot

on a private shoal of ground stones
we watched the stars vanish as the light
of the world rose slowly from the great
gray inland sea. Wet, shivering, raised
our beer cans to the long seasons
to come. We would never die.
                              Scattered
to distant shores, long ago gone back
to the oily earth of Ohio,
the carved Kentucky hills, the smokeless air.

28

At 28 I was still faithless.
I had crossed the country in a green Ford,
sleeping one night almost 14 hours in a motel
above Salt Lake City. I discovered
I'd had a fever all that day and thus the animals
that dotted the road, the small black spots
that formed and unformed crows, the flying pieces
of slate that threatened to break through
the windshield . . . were whatever they were.
I took two aspirins and an allergy pill—that was all
I had—and got into bed although it was light out.
That was 28 years ago. Since then I have died
only twice, once in slow motion against
the steel blue driver's side of a Plymouth
station wagon. One moment before impact I said
to myself, seriously, "This is going to hurt."
The kids in the Plymouth's back seat gaped
wildly, shouted, leaped, and the father held firm
to the steering wheel as I slipped through the space
that was theirs, untouched, skidding first
on the black field of asphalt and broken glass
that is California 168, Tollhouse Road, and over
the edge of the mountain, the motorcycle
tumbling off on its own through nettles and grass
to come to a broken rest as all bodies must.
Often when I shave before a late dinner, especially
on summer evenings, I notice the white lines
on my right shoulder like the smeared imprint
of a leaf on silk or the delicate tracings
on a whale's fins that the smaller sea animals carve
to test his virtue, and I reenter the wide blue eyes
of that family of five that passed on their way
up the mountain.
                    But at 28 I was still faithless.
I could rise before dawn from a bed drenched
with my own sweat, repack the green Ford
in the dark, my own breath steaming

in the high, clear air, and head for California.
I could spend the next night in Squaw Valley
writing a letter to my wife and kids asleep hours
behind me in Colorado, I could listen to Rexroth
reminiscing on a Berkeley FM station in the voice
God uses to lecture Jesus Christ and still believe
two aspirins, an allergy pill, and proper rest were proof
against the cold that leaps in one blind moment
from the heart to the farthest shore to shudder
through the small sea creatures I never knew existed.

It seems the sun passing back and forth behind clouds
this morning threatens to withdraw its affections
and the sky is as distant and pale as a bored child
in the wrong classroom or a man of 28
drilled so often on the names of fruit-bearing trees
that he forgets even the date palm. Here in New England,
no longer new or English, the first frost
has stained the elms and maples outside my window,
and the kids on their way hunch their shoulders
against the cold. One boy drops his lunch box
with a clatter and mysteriously leaves it there
on the pavement as a subtle rebuke
to his mother, to a father holding tight to a wheel,
to a blue Plymouth that long ago entered the heaven
brooding above Detroit. If only they had stopped
all those years ago and become a family of five
descending one after the other the stone ledges
of Sweet Potato Mountain and found me face down
among the thistles and shale and lifted me to my feet.
I weighed no more than feathers do or the wish
to become pure spirit. If I had not broken my glasses
I could have gone on my way with a thank you,
with a gap-toothed smile.
                    28 years ago, faithless, I
found the great bay of San Francisco where the map
said it would be and crossed the bridge from Oakland

singing "I Cover the Waterfront" into the cold winds
and the dense odor of coffee. Before I settled
in East Palo Alto among divorcees and appliance salesmen,
fifty yards from the Union Pacific tracks, I spent a long weekend
with Arthur, my mentor to be. In a voice ruined, he said,
by all-night draughts of whiskey and coffee, he praised
the nobility of his lemon and orange trees, the tang
of his loquats, the archaic power of his figs.
In a gambler's green visor and stiff Levis, he bowed
to his wounded tomatoes swelling into late summer.
Kneeling in the parched loam by the high fence
he bared the elusive strawberries, his blunt fingers
working the stiff leaves over and over. It was August.
He was almost happy.
                    Faithless, I had not found
the olive trees bursting on the hillsides west
of US 99. I knew only the bitter black fruit
that clings with all its life to the hard seed.
I had not wakened to mockers wrangling in my yard
at dawn in a riot of sexual splendor or heard
the sea roar at Bondy Bay, the long fingers
of ocean running underneath the house all night
to rinse off the pain of nightmare. I had not
seen my final child, though he was on the way.
I had not become a family of five nor opened
my arms to receive the black gifts of a mountain road,
of ground cinders, pebbles, rough grass.
                                        At twice my age
Arthur, too, was faithless, or so he insisted
through the long sober evenings in Los Altos, once
crowded with the cries of coyotes. His face
darkened and his fists shook when he spoke
of Nothing, what he would become in that waiting blaze
of final cold, a whiteness like no other.
At 56, more scared of me than I of him,
his right forefinger raised to keep the beat,
he gravelled out his two great gifts of truth:

"I'd rather die than reread the last novels
of Henry James," and, "Philip, we must never lie
or we shall lose our souls." All one winter afternoon
he chanted in Breton French the coarse poems of Tristan Corbière,
his voice reaching into unforeseen sweetness, both hands
rising toward the ceiling, the tears held back so long
still held back, for he was dying and he was ready.

By April I had crossed the Pacheco Pass and found
roosting in the dark branches of the Joshua tree
the fabled magpie— "Had a long tongue and a long tail;
He could both talk and do." This is a holy land,
I thought. At a Sonoco station the attendant,
wiry and dour, said in perfect Okie, "Be careful, son,
a whole family was wiped out right here
just yesterday." At Berenda the fields flooded
for miles in every direction. Arthur's blank sky
stared down at an unruffled inland sea and threatened
to let go. On the way home I cut lilacs
from the divider strip of El Camino Real.
My wife was pregnant. All night we hugged
each other in our narrow bed as the rain
came on in sheets. A family of five, and all
of us were out of work. The dawn was silent.
The black roses, battered, unclenched, the burned petals
floated on the pond beside the playhouse.
Beneath the surface the tiny stunned pike circled
no prey we could see. That was not another life.
I was 29 now and faithless, not the father of the man
I am but the same man who all this day
sat in a still house watching the low clouds massing
in the west, the new winds coming on.
By late afternoon the kids are home from school,
clambering on my front porch, though day
after day I beg them not to. When I go
to the window they race off in mock horror,
daring me to follow. The huge crows that wake

me every morning settle back on the rain spout
next door to caw to the season. I could put them
all in a poem, title it "The Basket of Memory"
as though each image were an Easter egg waiting to hatch,
as though I understood the present and the past
or even why the 8 year old with a cap of blond hair
falling to her shoulders waves to me as she darts
between parked cars and cartwheels into the early dusk.

THESE STREETS

If I told you that the old woman
named Ida Bellow was shot to death
for no more than $5 and that a baby
of eighteen months saw it all from
where she wakened on the same bed
but can't tell because she can't speak,
you'd say I was making it up. If I
took you by the hand and led you down
street after street until we arrived
at a door that seemed no different
from the rest and entered to behold
the flowered coverlet not yet washed
on the single iron bed, the calendar
stopped on the second Sunday in February,
the cluttered three-burner stove, the sink
of cracked dishes, the old wheelchair
Ida used to get around, you'd stand
in the middle of the bare floor as far
from everything as you could get
listening to the cracked window moan
and see nothing. The baby's mother—
she's only nineteen—says she'll raise
the baby by herself now Ida's gone,
and she's not going to cry about it,
no, not in front of us two. No.
It was Cabin, the neighbor lady says,
Ida raised him from a child, raised
him up to this, and raised his sisters,
too, and she counts them off on her fingers,
one, two, three, four, she counts them off.

*

Why did we come here to begin with?
There was a pond once, and a path
small creatures took into the woods.
Brown warblers called down the first light,

271

and we woke with it to the long days
bursting with sudden anemones, iris
growing wild, purple throated finches
as small as canaries tumbling the air.
In late summer tall grasses grew, and we
hid side by side from the heavy sun, hid
in our own neat bed of broken reeds,
a little cup the earth made for us.
Our breath came and went. The sky passed
overhead still unstreaked by the geese
heading down from Canada, unmarred
by anything except the clouds massing
toward late afternoon. Yes, it was August
once, and the west wind was warm, even
at sunset. When I closed my eyes I
slept, when I opened them I saw a river
of stars overflowing their black bowl.

*

Six floor walk-ups, half the windows
boarded up, the doorways bricked over.
Still some families hanging on, kids
flood into the ruined streets morning
after morning on their way to school.
When it dies down, stray animals pick
over the rubbish, a family of four cats
exits the innards of a blooming sofa.
Between 9:30 and afternoon not
a single car starts up or passes down
the street. In the corner grocery
three lopsided apples on special,
30 cents each. The woman says it's
a good neighborhood, ain't no violence
here, ain't no trouble. A man comes
out of the back room and stares
at me until I look away. No one

speaks, not even the radio. The light
of the world filters down from shelves
of Brillo, bright packages of detergent,
paper diapers, roach motels, white
stale saltless crackers. Moment
by yellow moment the day ticks into
the past, and no one tries anything.

DOG POEM

Fierce and stupid all dogs are
and some worse. I learned this
early by walking to school
unarmed and unprepared
for big city life, which they
had been bred to for centuries.
The chow who barred my way
snarling through his black lips
taught me I was tiny and helpless
and that if he grew more determined
I could neither talk nor fight,
and my school books, my starred exams,
my hand-woven woolen mittens, a gift
of my grandmother, would fall
to the puddled sidewalk and
at best my cold sack of lunch
might buy me a few moments
to prepare my soul before I slept.
I inched by him, smelling the breath
hot and sour as old clothes.
He did nothing but rave, rising
toward me on his hind legs
and choking against the collar
which miraculously held. Later,
years later, delivering mail
on bicycle in the new California,
I was set on by a four-footed moron
who tore at my trousers even
as I drummed small rocks off
his head. I dreamed that head
became soup, and the small eyes stared
out into the bright dining room
of the world's great dog lovers,
and they ate and wept by turns
while I pedaled through the quiet streets
bringing bad news and good to
the dogless citizenry of Palo Alto.

The shepherd dog without sheep
who guards the gates to sleep wakens
each night as my tiny boat
begins to drift out on the waters
of silence. He bays and bays
until the lights come on, and I
sit up sweating and alarmed, alone
in the bed I came to call home.
Now I am weary of fighting and carry
at all times small hard wafers
of dried essence of cat to purchase
a safe way among the fanged masters
of the avenues. If I must come back
to this world let me do so as the lion
of legend, but striped like an alley cat.
Let me saunter back the exact way
I came turning each corner to face
the barking hosts of earth until they
scurry for cover or try pathetically
to climb the very trees that earlier
they peed upon and shamed. Let their pads
slide upon the glassy trunks,
weight them down with exercise books,
sacks of post cards, junk mail, ads,
dirty magazines, give them three kids
in the public schools, hemorrhoids,
a tiny fading hope to rise above
the power of unleashed, famished animals
and postmasters, give them two big feet
and shoes that don't fit, and dull work
five days a week. Give them my life.

A THEORY OF PROSODY

When Nellie, my old pussy
cat, was still in her prime,
she would sit behind me
as I wrote, and when the line
got too long she'd reach
one sudden black foreleg down
and paw at the moving hand,
the offensive one. The first
time she drew blood I learned
it was poetic to end
a line anywhere to keep her
quiet. After all, many morn-
ings she'd gotten to the chair
long before I was even up.
Those nights I couldn't sleep
she'd come and sit in my lap
to calm me. So I figured
I owed her the short cat line.
She's dead now almost nine years,
and before that there was one
during which she faked attention
and I faked obedience.
Isn't that what it's about—
pretending there's an alert cat
who leaves nothing to chance.

A WALK WITH TOM JEFFERSON

Between the freeway
          and the gray conning towers
of the ballpark, miles
          of mostly vacant lots, once
a neighborhood of small
          two-storey wooden houses—
dwellings for immigrants
          from Ireland, Germany,
Poland, West Virginia,
          Mexico, Dodge Main.
A little world with only
          three seasons, or so we said—
one to get tired, one to get
          old, one to die.
No one puts in irises,
          and yet before March passes
the hard green blades push
          their way through
where firm lawns once were.
          The trunks of beech and locust
darken, the light new branches
          take the air. You can
smell the sticky sap rising
          in the maples, smell it
even over the wet stink
          of burned houses.
On this block seven houses
          are still here to be counted,
and if you count the shacks
          housing illegal chickens,
the pens for dogs, the tiny
          pig sty that is half cave . . .
and if you count them you can
          count the crows' nest
in the high beech tree
          at the corner, and you can
regard the beech tree itself

bronzing in mid-morning light
as the mast of the great ship
    sailing us all back
into the 16th century
    or into the present age's
final discovery. (Better
    perhaps not to speak
of final anything, for
    this place was *finally* retired,
the books thrown away
    when after the town exploded
in '67 these houses
    were plundered for whatever
they had. Some burned
    to the ground, some
hung open, doorless, wide-eyed
    until hauled off
by the otherwise unemployable
    citizens of the county
to make room for the triumphant
    return of Mad Anthony Wayne,
Père Marquette, Cadillac,
    the badger, the wolverine,
the meadow lark, the benign
    long toothed bi-ped
with nothing on his mind.)
    During baseball season
the neighborhood's a thriving
    business for anyone
who can make change
    and a cardboard sign
that reads "Parking $3."
    He can stand on the curb
directing traffic and pretending
    the land is his.
On August nights I come
    out here after ten

and watch the light rise
        from the great gray bowl
of the stadium, watch it catch
        a scrap of candy wrapper
in the wind, a soiled napkin
        or a peanut shell and turn
it into fire or the sound
        of fire as the whole world
holds its breath. In the last
        inning 50,000
pulling at the night
        air for one last scream.
They can drain the stars
        of light. No one
owns any of this.
        It's condemned,
but the money for the execution
        ran out years ago.
Money is a dream, part
        of the lost past.
Joe Louis grew up a few miles
        east of here and attended
Bishop Elementary.
        No one recalls
a slender, dumbfounded
        boy afraid of his fifth grade
home room teacher. Tom Jefferson
        —"Same name as the other one"—
remembers Joe at seventeen
        all one sweltering summer
unloading bales of rags
        effortlessly from the trucks
that parked in the alley
        behind Wolfe Sanitary Wiping Cloth.
"Joe was beautiful,"
        is all he says, and we two
go dumb replaying Joe's

glide across the ring
as he corners Schmeling
        and prepares to win
World War II. Like Joe
        Tom was up from Alabama,
like Joe he didn't talk
        much then, and even now
he passes a hand across
        his mouth when speaking
of the $5 day that lured
        his father from the cotton fields
and a one-room shack the old folks
        talked about until
they went home first
        to visit and later to die.
Early afternoon behind
        his place, Tom's gathering up
the remnants of this year's
        garden—the burned
tomato plants and the hardy
        runners of summer squash
that dug into the chalky
        soil and won't let go.
He stuffs the dried remains
        into a supermarket shopping cart
to haul off to an empty block.
        The zinnias are left,
the asters in browns and dirty
        yellows, tough petalled
autumn blooms, even a few
        sticky green rose buds
climbing a telephone pole.
        Alabama is not so far back
it's lost in a swirl
        of memory. "I can see trees
behind the house. I do
        believe I still feel

winter mornings, all of us
        getting up from one bed
but for what I don't know."
        He tips his baseball cap
to the white ladies passing
        back the way we've come.
"We all come for $5
        a day and we got this!"
His arms spread wide to
        include block after block
of dumping grounds,
        old couches and settees
burst open, the white innards
        gone gray, cracked
and mangled chifforobes
        that long ago gave up
their secrets, yellow wooden
        ice boxes yawning
at the sky, their breath
        still fouled with years
of eating garlic sausage
        and refried beans,
the shattered rib cages
        of beds that couldn't hold
our ordinary serviceable dreams,
        blue mattresses stained
in earnest, the cracked
        toilet seats of genius,
whole market counters
        that once contained the red meats
we couldn't get enough of,
        burned out electric motors,
air conditioners
        we suffocated, and over all
an arctic wind from Canada
        which carries off
the final faint unseeable

spasm of the desire
to be human and brings down
the maple and elm leaves
of early October. If you follow
their trail of burnished arrows
scuttling across curbs and cracked
sidewalks they'll lead
you to the cellar hole
of something or someone
called Dogman. "Making do,"
says Tom Jefferson.
His neighbors swear
someone runs on all fours
with his dog packs. They claim
they can tell when
their own dogs feel the pull
of the wild ones.
The women talk of lost
house cats grown to the size
of cougars. They've heard them
crashing through the dense
underbrush of the dumping
ground and found
huge paw tracks in the snow,
the remains of drunks
and children caught out
after dark, nothing but clean bones
revealed under ice when
the spring rains come back.
"There ain't no kids
around here," says Tom,
"But if there were, the bones
be about the same size."
Tom has seen vapor rising
through the missing floorboards,
clouds of it, and maybe
animals and man

together producing a new
                variety of steam heat.
Even I have seen a brutish
                black mongrel Dane
in late afternoon, his coat
                snow flecked, rising
on his hind legs to over
                seven feet, hanging
over fences, peering in windows
                as though he yearned
to come back to what
                we were. Winter's in everything
we say— it's coming on—we see
                it in the mad swirl
of leaves and newspapers
                doing their dances.
We feel it as iron
                in the wind. We could escape,
each of us feels in
                his shuddering heart, take
the bridge south to Canada,
                but we don't. Instead we
hunker down, slump a little
                lower in our trousers,
and go slow. One night soon
                I'll waken to a late quiet
and go out to see all this
                transformed, each junked car,
each dumping ground and battered
                hovel a hill
of mounded snow, every scrap
                of ugliness redeemed
under the light of a street lamp
                or the moon. From the dark tower
of the Renaissance Center Ford built
                to look down
on our degradation to the great

Ford plant downriver blowing
its black breath in the face
        of creation, the one at Rouge
where he broke first our backs
        and then the rest, everything
silent, suspended in a new world
        like no other. For a moment
a few stars come out to share
        this witness. I won't believe it,
but Tom will. Tom Jefferson
        is a believer.
You can't plant winter vegetables
        if you aren't,
you can't plant anything, except
        maybe radishes.
You don't have to believe
        anything to grow
radishes. Early August he's got
        sweet corn
two feet above his head,
        he stretches
his arm to show where
        they grow to.
Tomatoes "remind you what tomatoes
        taste like."
He was planting before the Victory Gardens.
        His mother brought
the habit up from Alabama. She was
        growing greens
behind the house no matter how small
        her strip of land,
cosmos beside the back door,
        early things
like pansies along the fence.
        "Why she could go
into a bare field and find
        the purple flags,

wild, bring them home, half-
    dead dirty chicks
on the palm of her hand, and they'd
    grow. I could
never do that, I gave up trying
    fifty years ago."
It didn't take FDR
    and "the war effort"
to make a believer out of Tom.
    When he went off to war
his son Tom Jr. took over
    the garden and did
a job, the same son went off
    to Korea and didn't
come home, the son he seldom talks
    about, just as he
seldom talks about his three years
    in the Seabees
building airstrips so we could
    bomb Japan, doing
the war work he did at home
    for less pay.
A father puts down a spade, his son
    picks it up,
"That's Biblical," he says,
    "the son goes off,
the father takes up the spade
    again, that's Biblical."
He'd leave for work in the cold
    dark of December.
Later, out the high broken windows
    at Dodge Main
he'd see the snow falling
    silently and know
it was falling on the dark petals
    of the last rose,
know his wife was out

                              back hunched
              in her heavy gray sweater
                              letting those first flakes
              slowly settle into
                              water on the warm
              red flesh of the dime store
                              plants Tom Jr.
              put in on his own.
                              Later he'd come home
              in the early dark
                              with snow on his hair,
              tracking the dirty
                              snow on her rug—
              they say the dogs yellow
                              it before it hits
              the ground—and she would
                              say nothing.
              "That's Biblical," he says.
                              "We couldn't even look
              near each other
                              for fear of how
              one might make the other cry.
                              That's Biblical,
              knowing the other so well
                              you know yourself,
              being careful the way she was
                              never to say nothing
              or show the least sign."
                              Tom picks a maple leaf
              stiff backed and brown
                              from the gutter,
              holds it against the distant
                              pale sky streaked
              with contrails. Maybe even
                              war is Biblical, maybe
              even the poor white
                              fighting the poor black

in this city for the same
        gray concrete housing,
the same gray jobs
        they both came
north for, maybe that's
        Biblical, the way
the Canaanites and the Philistines
        fought the Israelites,
and the Israelites killed
        the Amalakites
always for the same land.
        "God wanted Saul
to kill them down to the last lamb.
        He didn't,
and he went crazy. Back
        in the riots of '42
they did not kill us down
        to the last lamb.
They needed us making airfields
        the way they needed us
making Fords before the war,
        maybe that's why
they went crazy." There at the end
        of the street is his house,
his since he came home
        and could never leave.
The wisteria along the side
        has grown to the thickness
of his own wrist, the back yard
        is roses still, squash
coming on, onions in late
        bloom to be tricked
by the first cold, potatoes
        hidden underground,
they think, forever.
        "It's Biblical.
The way David plays for Saul so he

can weep, and later
when his turn comes David
weeps for Absalom.
It's Biblical, you cry,
it's Biblical you don't,
either way. That's Biblical."
What commandment
was broken to bring God's
wrath down on these streets,
what did we wrong, going
about our daily lives,
to work at all hours until
the work dried up,
then sitting home until home
became a curse
with the yellow light
of afternoon falling
with all the weight of final
judgement, I can't say.
It's Biblical, this season
of color coming
to its end, the air swirling
in tiny cyclones
of brown and red, the air
swelling my lungs,
banging about my ears so that
I almost think I hear
Tom say "Absalom" again, a name
owed to autumn
and the autumn of his hopes.
It's Biblical,
the little pyres pluming
the afternoon gray and blue
on these corners, the calm
of these childless streets,
a dog howling from a distant
block, another answering,

the calls of the chained animals
      going back and forth
so plaintive and usual no one
      hears. The sparrows
fan out across the grassless yards
      busily seeking
whatever seeds the cold winds
      burst forth, and this
day is coming to its end
      with only the smallest
winter birds to keep
      the vigil. "We need
this season," Tom has said,
      but Tom believes
the roots need cold,
      the earth needs to turn
to ice and snow so a new fire
      can start up in the heart
of all that grows.
      He doesn't say that.
He doesn't say the heart
      of ice is fire waiting,
he doesn't say the new seed
      nestles in the old,
waiting, frozen, for the land
      to thaw, and even these streets
of cracking blacktop long gone gray,
      the seven junked cars
the eye can note collapsed
      on slashed tires, their insides
drawn out for anything, he doesn't
      say all this is a lost land,
it's Biblical. He parks his chromed
      shopping cart under the porch,
brushes the dirt and leaves
      from his worn corduroy—
six feet of man, unbowed—

and locks the knee-high gate
of his fence that could
        hold back no one,
smiles and says the one word,
        "Tomorrow," and goes in.
Later he'll put the porch light on,
        though no one's coming.
The crazy Indian colors
        are blooming as the sun
begins to go, deep maroons
        they tell us are the signs
of all the earth we've pumped
        into the sky.
The same rich browns the ground
        reveals after rain,
the veins of orange I've uncovered
        digging the yard
spring after spring. Never once
        have I found the least sign
that this was once the Indian's
        ground, perhaps a holy land,
not a single arrow head
        or shard, though I
have caught a sudden glint of
        what I didn't know
while turning over dirt I swore
        was never turned before
only to kneel to a bottle cap
        polished down
to anonymity or a wad
        of tinfoil
from an empty pack
        of Luckys, curled
to the shape of whatever
        vanished human hand
tossed it off. We were not
        idle hands. Still a kid

when I worked nights
       on the milling machines
at Cadillac transmission,
       another kid just up
from West Virginia asked me
       what was we making,
and I answered, I'm making
       2.25 an hour,
don't know what you're
       making, and he had
to correct me, gently, what was
       we making out of
this here metal, and I didn't know.
       Whatever it was we
made, we made of earth. Amazing earth,
       amazed perhaps
by all it's given us,
       as amazed as I
who stood one afternoon
       forty years ago
at a railroad crossing
       near Joy Road
as the Sherman tanks passed
       two to a flat-bed car,
on their way to a war,
       their long guns
frowning down identically, they
       passed some twenty minutes
or more while the tracks groaned,
       the trestle snapped
and sighed with so much stubborn
       weight of our going.
Later, in the forge room
       at Chevy, now a man,
still making what I never knew,
       I stood in the silence
of the great presses slamming

home, the roar of earth
striking the fired earth, the reds
          searing their glowing image
into the eye and brain,
          the oranges and roses
blooming in the mind long
          after, even in sleep.
What were we making out
          of this poor earth good
for so much giving and taking?
          (Beets the size of fists
by the thousands, cabbages
          as big as brains
year after year, whole cribs
          of peppers, great lakes
of sweet corn tumbling
          by the trailer load,
it gave and gave, and whatever
          we had it took.)
The place was called Chevy
          Gear & Axle—
it's gone now, gone to earth
          like so much here—
so perhaps we actually made
          gears and axles
for the millions of Chevies
          long dead or still to die.
It said that, "Chevrolet
          Gear & Axle"
right on the checks they paid
          us with, so I can
half-believe that's what we
          were making way back then.

A NOTE ABOUT THE AUTHOR

Philip Levine was born in 1928 in Detroit and was formally educated there, at the public schools and at Wayne State University. After a succession of industrial jobs he left the city for good and lived in various parts of the country before settling in Fresno, California, where he now teaches. *The Names of the Lost* won the Lenore Marshall Award for the best book of poetry published by an American in 1976. Three of his books have been nominated for the National Book Critics Circle Award, and two of them, *Ashes* and *7 Years from Somewhere*, have received it. *Ashes* also received the American Book Award in 1980. In 1987 he received the Ruth Lilly Poetry Prize "for distinguished poetic achievements," awarded by *Poetry* magazine and The American Council for the Arts. His *New Selected Poems* (which replaces the earlier *Selected Poems* of 1984) was published simultaneously with *What Work Is*, which won the National Book Award for Poetry in 1991. *The Simple Truth* was awarded the Pulitzer Prize in Poetry in 1995.

A NOTE ON THE TYPE

This book was set in Monticello, a Linotype revival of the original Roman No. 1 cut by Archibald Binny and cast in 1796 by the Philadelphia type foundry Binny & Ronaldson. The face was named Monticello in honor of its use in the monumental fifty-volume *Papers of Thomas Jefferson*, published by Princeton University Press. Monticello is a transitional type design, embodying certain features of Bulmer and Baskerville, but it is a distinguished face in its own right.

Composition by Heritage Printers, Inc., Charlotte, N.C.
Printed and bound by Kingsport Press
Kingsport, Tennessee
Designed by Harry Ford

9014